Healing Affirmations for the Wounded Soul

Melissa Jones

PublishAmerica

Baltimore

First printing

ISBN: 1-4137-6052-X
PUBLISHED BY PUBLISHAMERICA, LLLP
www.publishamerica.com
Baltimore

Printed in the United States of America

Dedication

I dedicate this book to my two beautiful daughters Jasmine and Nia. Jasmine, the moment I looked into your eyes, I fell in love with you. Nia, when I looked into your eyes, I knew that you were blessed with the same gifts as Mommy. Nia, it is because I chose to give you life, my life began to fill with purpose. Words can never describe my love for you two. I pray this book of my life lessons will encourage you to make wise decisions. I pray this book will be a guide for you as you grow up. It is my prayer the affirmations written in it will help you speak the will of the Almighty God into your lives. I also pray this book will direct you towards a journey of success and a life full of love by affirming the fruits of the Spirit into the depths of your precious souls. Mommy says to you a word of wisdom: *I applied my heart to what I observed and learned a lesson from what I saw* (Proverbs 24;32). Always remember the blessing in the gift of life is freewill. Dream big, and use the greatest gift you have (your faith) to make them come true!

Love,
Mommy

Acknowledgments

I acknowledge God, my creator, without whom I am nothing. Thank you, Father, for being so patient with me while I worked through all my dysfunctional behaviors. Through it all, you have loved me. Because of your unfailing love, my soul has been filled with much gratitude.

I would also like to acknowledge Iyanla Vanzant, who undoubtedly helped me tap into the deep powers of my spirit. Your books and tapes have helped me advance to a level of awareness I could have never discovered without your words of wisdom.

I would also like to acknowledge Trina Henderson, who has always supported me. Your encouraging words and support have been a blessing to me. Thank you for believing in me.

I would also like to acknowledge the Tabernacle Baptist Church of Atlanta, Georgia, where I was taught the commandment of love; Second Mount Vernon Baptist Church (East) of Atlanta, Georgia, where I came to know my true purpose for being alive; and World Changers Church located in College Park, Georgia, where I have been taught the laws of faith and prosperity. I acknowledge each of these leaders and thank them dearly for each seed they have planted into my life concerning the word of God.

To my dear friend Derek James: I remember the first day I met you. I needed to use your library card to check out a book. You did not know me, but you trusted me. Thank you. You have always listened to my wild faith stories and laughed at each one. Thank you for listening. Whenever I need you, you are always there. Thank you for being a true friend. Your love and support throughout the years have meant so much to me. May God pour a one hundred-fold blessing upon your life for your kindness towards my children and I. We love you!

Daddy,

I hope you enjoy reading my book. People change, as do the seasons. I want you to know that I understand you did the best you could while taking care of us. I know you have always loved me, and I know I deeply hurt you on my journey towards growth. The love of God has infused my soul and has healed me of my troubled past. I hope all the hurt and tears I have caused you can now be transformed into joy and happiness. I love you, Daddy!

Mom,

God has forgiven you, I have forgiven you, Tiki has forgiven you, and Sammy has forgiven you. It is okay to forgive yourself. I love you. Thank you for nourishing me inside of your womb. Thank you for the gift of life. Without you, I could not have been brought forth into this world to fulfill my purpose.

Pastor Robert (Bob) Tilton (Word of Faith Ministries),

Without your letters of faith, I could not have held on. I remember there were days when I was ready to throw in the towel, and then, I would check my mailbox, and an anointed letter written specifically for my circumstances waited for me. Thank you for encouraging me and covering me with your many prayers. Your partnership letters have helped me through many rough times. I love you, Pastor Bob! You were right. I am a child of God! I am so blessed to be partners with you in ministry.

To my patients living with AIDS at Grady Memorial Infectious Disease Clinic in Atlanta Georgia,

You all are so strong. To arise each day and make efforts to come and take care of your health in spite of the odds you face, inspires me . I enjoy serving you, listening to you, praying with you and for you, and most of all, I enjoy seeing to it that you get the proper medications to help keep you alive. Keep on fighting. All of you are truly survivors and I just admire your strength and your courage! May God bless and keep you always.

From the Author

I wrote this book hoping to inspire those who desire to have an intimate experience with God. Religion can confuse many people due to the demands of others' beliefs and all the man-made ideas that people come up with to satisfy their own personal fulfillments. As I grow in God every day, I realize that religion only places God in a sealed up box. God is so much bigger than religion. I feel that if one believes in his heart and confesses with his mouth that God gave His only begotten son so that he may have a chance to inherit eternal life, he then has become a child of the most high and will gain eternal life through our Lord and Savior, Jesus Christ.

I also believe that if one is to become a disciple of Jesus then he must keep faith, love, and hope alive in his heart and obey the leading of the Holy Spirit. I also believe we must learn to become genuine people of faith. It is time for Christians to stop putting on an act by pretending that being a disciple of Jesus Christ is one of the most pleasant experiences one could have. People who desire to walk with Jesus need to know the truth. This is the truth: walking with God is indeed one of the most rewarding experiences one can ever have while walking the grounds of this earth, yet there are many painful trials and tests that come with the walk. Many have turned away from God because of them, and many overcome them.

I desire to share my experiences with you so that you may begin to feel comfortable with who and where you are in this world as a Christian. I also want to come clean and share my joys and failures with you so that you may have a better understanding that there are many trials and tests in the lives of Christians, and the journey of a Christian is difficult, but God always works things out as long as we do not give up. The truth is that people who walk with God make mistakes each and every day just as someone who knows nothing about Him. People who love and serve God are by no means perfect. God did not design life to be perfect. He desires us to strive for perfection depending totally on His strength at all times.

God designed trials and tribulations to perfect your faith, to develop perseverance and character, and to prepare you to spend eternal life with Him. The trials and tribulations that you face here on earth somehow perfect your inner self. When tests and trials come, they make you spiritually strong. Some trials are designed to teach you about faith, and some are designed to teach you patience. There are many lessons to be learned from our trials and tests. The most important lesson God would have you learn is Love. Love is to be learned and practiced with every lesson, every trial, and every test.

Because love is the greatest commandment, God will give you many chances and several experiences to master it. If you do not learn how to develop love in your heart, then there is no way you can ever have an experience with God. Truthfully, there is no way you will ever see God. It is very important you begin today to ask your self this question: Through all my experiences, trials, and tests, how has God tried to teach me the true meaning of love? I encourage you to begin to keep a journal and write all of your experiences and the lessons that you have learned, in it. Also record what spiritual principle you have mastered with each experience. When it is your appointed time to meet God, He is going to want to know how you have demonstrated love towards Him, yourself, and others while you walked the face of this earth.

I also wrote this book to give you an inside scoop of just how imperfect a Christian can be, but with willingness, patience, and a whole lot of prayer, God can shape the most nutty Christian into a beautiful image of Himself. That is why God is the potter and you and I are the clay. With each experience we have, God molds us into the people He desires us to be. Would a potter who has a perfect piece of clay keep on working with it? No, he would leave it alone and get it ready to be sold. The piece of clay has no definition until the potter begins to roll it around in his hands. As he rolls it and plays with it, he begins to get ideas and images for this piece of clay. He begins to give it a shape and makes a beautiful piece of art out of clay. When a potter molds a piece of clay, he keeps on working with it by shaping it with his hands until he thinks it is perfect (in his eyes).

God has a vision for our lives, and in order to make the vision happen, He must shape us into men and women of God. This takes time, and it does not happen overnight. Sometimes it takes years for God to work with us. He shapes us by presenting us with different experiences to develop our faith, our love, our character, and to give us hope. He is constantly rolling us around in His hands, making sure we are formed into beautiful pieces of art.

Loving God is not about doing everything right. It is actually about doing everything wrong, so that you may learn how to do right. As you read this book, I pray you will be inspired to become a free, honest, and open-minded Christian. You will read about many exciting things I have experienced while walking with God. Many Christians believe that a self-righteous attitude makes them right with God, but I have learned that faith, love, and hope make you right with Him. I do not care how holy and self-righteous you may think you are, if you do not have faith, love, or hope inside of your heart, you are not right with God.

Those three things have seemed to remain when all else has appeared to fail in my life. When everything looked as though it was coming apart, I always believed someday things would get better. I recall that each time I was faced with trouble, I would tell God: "Lord, if you can just help me through this problem, I will be all right." After each problem seemed to be solved, another one surfaced. I do not tell God that anymore. Now, I ask God to give me wisdom to learn the lesson, the power to sustain me, to teach me to love and forgive more, and to prepare me for the next lesson.

No matter how difficult my situations became, I never stopped believing that God loved and cared for me. I believed that no matter what happened to me, God would deliver me from all my troubles. I did my best to keep love alive in my heart, and I did not allow the hurt and pain others caused me and those I caused myself to make me bitter and resentful. I made a choice to love God no matter what and to love others in spite of it all. When others mistreated me, I learned to forgive them, separate from them, and pray for them. I guess by offering a simple prayer for others, it somehow kept my heart tender and merciful towards people. Each day, I hoped for brighter days. I can remember thinking that I was one day closer to discovering my purpose here on earth. I also remember affirming to myself repeatedly that things were getting better and my life was actually changing. Now when I look back, I am so glad that I affirmed those things because my life did change for the better.

I do not know how you feel, but I enjoy reading books that inspire me to keep pressing on along this journey called life. I like reading testimonies about people who have had an experience with our creator God. I love reading about people who have overcome their challenges in life. I have always read throughout my bible that God would deliver the needy when he cries unto him. I also remember reading He would set the poor on high from their afflictions. I discovered that God has prepared goodness for the poor. I somehow believed the one whom God was referring to as " poor," was me. I entered into this big world destined to be afflicted, destined to be hurt, destined to suffer, but now, I know that it is only through my suffering I am raised up to a higher level of spirituality, teaching me to love in spite of my circumstances. I have learned that through all of my suffering, I was able to identify with the Lord Jesus Christ.

God loves to do the impossible in peoples lives. He loves raising those who are lowly in spirit. God likes to shed his grace on people who are wounded and hurt. I understand the odds of me becoming a survivor of my past were very slim. I know that society says people with pasts such as mines are likely to end up drug addicted, mentally insane, or destined for a road of failure due to the emotional and mental damage that takes place in their lives. I am thankful that in spite of all I have been through, I have survived to share my testimony with others. I have learned very important lessons about love, peace, patience, forgiveness, perseverance, and hope. My soul always desired to be put together to be made whole, so that I may one day stand before God ready to spend eternity in His presence. I believe God is finally bringing my inner self into a complete balance, and each day I am becoming whole.

I pray this book will bless your life. I pray that you begin to see your life and the lessons presented to you as an avenue to eternity and spiritual growth and not as a punishment from God. I also pray that if you are one who has spent most of your life feeling shattered in your soul due to negative circumstances you have encountered, you would use the affirmations written in this book and my testimony as a tool to help you begin, along with God's help, to put the shattered pieces together again. This book is based on my experience with God, and how He has revealed himself to me. This book tells how God stretched His hand out towards me and changed my life for the better. Many are the afflictions of the righteous, but the Lord does deliver him from them all. Let me encourage you to open your heart and mind as you read this book and allow your soul to be touched by the words written.

I also pray that His presence be revealed to you and you will allow Him to prepare you for eternal life. He has designed different experiences to present to you with many opportunities to make choices. It is remarkably interesting to know that whatever you choose to do in your decision making, God is always right there. Sometimes we may feel like we made bad choices in life, and we become angry with others and angry with God. Always remember God has given us the freedom to choose. I believe He granted us this freedom because it goes along with the gift of life. Who would want to come into this world and not be able to have the freedom to be that which he desires to be? Who would want to grow into an adult being forced to be something that he is not. That is not freedom. It is called bondage. God desires us to choose wisely, yet still, He knows that we all are going to make choices that cause some deep consequences in this lifetime.

Whatever we choose, God is always there. He is so patient with us. Sometimes we go through half of our lives being presented with different experiences, not learning the valuable lesson that God so desires for us to learn. We fail to carefully examine our circumstances and we end up going through the same things repeatedly. I have done this time after time, and yet, He always waited for me to get it together. Now that is patience. Let me encourage you today to stop! Begin to look at all of your present circumstances and situations and try to figure out what lesson is life trying to teach you.

Always choose to keep love alive in your heart no matter what. An opportunity to experience and practice love will always be presented in every experience you will ever have. When we consistently walk in love, we begin to realize that all of the other fruits of the Spirit begin to fall into the place where they belong and that is the very essence of your soul. I encourage you to begin to withdraw love from each and every experience you have, because it is through love that we are accepted by God and through love, you will be totally prepared to enter into eternity at your appointed time. While you are here on earth, learn to walk a life of love. If we desire spend eternity with God, then we must learn to love. And remember when all else fails these three remain: faith, love, and hope. God bless you, and I believe with faith that as you begin to reaffirm your life, wonderful changes will come.

Introduction
Becoming an Affirmer

You will make your prayer to Him, He will hear you and you will pay your vows. You will also declare a thing, and it will be established for you, so light will shine on your ways (Job22;27-28).

Have faith in God, I tell you the truth, if anyone says to this mountain, Go throw yourself in the sea, and does not doubt in his heart, but believes what he says will happen, it will be done for him. Therefore I tell you, whatever you ask for in prayer, believe that you have received it, and it will be yours (Mark 11;22-24).

An affirmer is someone who declares something aloud with their mouth that they believe to be true. An affirmer affirms what he believes to make that which he believes, manifest in his life. One becomes an affirmer by learning how to speak affirmations. An affirmation can also be a prayer offered in faith. You do not ask when you speak affirmations. You simply declare that which you desire in faith, believing that it will be done for you.

Let's use the creation as an example of an affirmation. The bible tells us that God spoke the universe into existence by His words. When God said, "Let there be light," there was light. Everything that God spoke, there was. The words "let there be" are an affirmation. Some may not be familiar with the word affirmation, but if we study our bible on the account of creation, we will then understand that God spoke our lovely universe into being through affirmations.

Since we are created in God's image, and because His divine spirit lives in us through every breath we take, we also have the ability to affirm something with the power of our words to make that which we believe manifest into reality. As Christians, we need to learn to use the power of our tongues to speak life into our situations. When we find ourselves in difficult situations, we must learn to speak life into them. When we find ourselves lacking confidence, we must learn to speak confidence into our lives. When our faith grows weary, we must learn to speak to the seed of faith that lies within us. No matter what situation you may find yourself in, you must learn to speak positive things into your life and speak negative things out of your life.

God has given you the ability to create your life by the thoughts you think, the words you speak, and the choices you make. I recall reading a book that described life as painting a picture. You can paint what ever you desire. You can use the colors you wish, and you can put anything your heart desires on that piece of paper to satisfy you. If you are not satisfied with the picture you have painted, then it is now time to paint a new one! You do have that right. The picture you have painted for your life may not be a picture you enjoy looking at every day, but you have the power inside of you to change it. With a fresh piece of paper, some brand new colors, the creativity of your mind, and the affirming power of your own words, you can begin to paint a new picture of your life. If you have not included God in your pictures of the past, then today would be a perfect day to begin. I challenge you to begin to acknowledge God and let Him be the main thing that stands out on your new picture of life. If God is in our picture, then we know that our new picture of life is now being painted with a purpose.

If you have not accepted the Lord Jesus Christ as your personal savior, I ask that you pray this short but powerful prayer with me now.

Father God, I acknowledge you as my creator, and I believe that you sent your son Jesus Christ to earth to die so that I may have life and have it abundantly. Today, I accept Jesus Christ as my personal savior, and I ask that today He make His home in my heart. I receive by faith Jesus Christ. I confess all my sins and believe in my heart they are forgiven. It is done!

Now you can go ahead and, visualize a brand new picture for your life. Forgive yourself for all of the negative things you have spoken from your mouth and begin to affirm love, forgiveness, success, good health, and wealth into your life. Use this book to help you begin to speak good things in your life. Begin to visualize the life you want for yourself and speak it into existence. Use new colors of love, forgiveness, confidence, trust, faith, hope, and perseverance to set a new atmosphere for your new picture of life. As you begin to learn to use the power of your tongue for goodness, you will see your life change drastically.

The word of God teaches us that in your tongue, you hold the power to speak life and death. The tongue is such a wonderful gift that has been imparted to us. This book will teach you how to begin to use the power of your tongue. This book is not one that you read once and store it in your closet! You must use it regularly. The affirmations are blessed and anointed by the Holy Spirit to help heal you and change your life. You may buy another copy for your friends and loved ones, but you must keep your copy and use it on a regular basis. I have prayed over the written affirmations and believe that they will tremendously change your life, if you speak them on a regular basis. And remember! Change does not happen over night. Change takes a lot of work and a lot of prayer. Be strong and very courageous, because God is with you wherever you go. When you take one step to reach out to God and change the way you think, speak, and act, God takes three steps towards you. Please have fun and be filled with zeal as you see your life change by affirming goodness into your life with the power of your own words. Affirm this prayer now to notify God of the changes you desire to make in your life through the words that you speak.

Father, I thank you that you have heard this affirming prayer, for I know that you always hear me when I pray. Today, I desire to change my life by the words I speak. I know that in the past I have spoken negative things about my situations. I ask for forgiveness, because somehow I did not realize my past and present circumstances possibly could have been better or can be better if I only begin to use my words correctly. I also forgive myself for the negative things I have spoken about others and myself. Today Lord, I am making a change by the words I speak, and with your ever present help, my life will change for the better. Today, I am looking forward to my life being changed by the power of my words. It is in your son Jesus Christ's name I pray, Amen.

From Darkness into God's Light

The lamp of the body is the eye. Therefore, if your eye is good, your whole body will be full of light, but if your eye is bad, your whole body will be full of darkness. If therefore the light that is in you is darkness, how great is that darkness (Matthew 6: 22-23).

Jesus Christ was an affirmer when He walked on the soils of this earth and still is as He exercises His earned rights of authority in heaven. So many people are unaware that they are gifted with this natural ability because they have not yet learned of their true identity. So many people are so overtaken by the cares of this world that they have been spiritually blind to the fact they are a representation of God. They walk this earth in darkness, not understanding their purpose for being here and become hopeless because they do not comprehend that because they are made like God and He lives in them through each breath they take, they have the power to accomplish many great things here on earth by using their words. I know, because I was one of those people.

Before I discovered who I really was, I actually believed I was a nobody. I felt worthless and lost. Because of my negative feelings towards myself, I was in darkness. I was blind to the fact that God planned a future for my life. I felt like I was destined for hurt, pain, and sadness. I subconsciously wanted to self-destruct so I used alcohol, cigarettes, sex, and my words to destroy myself. I was not aware at the time that I was engaging in self-destructive behavior because subconsciously, I wanted to die. Darkness is the path of evil, and I now know it was Satan, the father of lies and the ruler of darkness, who kept me in deception so he could slowly devour me and sift me as wheat, so that I would never come towards God's light to know the truth of myself.

As I began to study my bible, I slowly began to grasp the concept that I was a representation of God. I remember one night after I studied the creation of mankind I was tickled. I remember running to the mirror in the bathroom and staring at myself for a few moments. I had this bewildered look on my face as I studied the image in the mirror. I remember saying with a shallow voice and with a confused look on my face, "Lord, do I actually look like you?"

As I stared, I became full of joy. I remember putting a smile on my face and saying, "Well, God, if I look like you, then I need to start acting like you."

It was at that point my life began to change. From that evening on, I began to meditate on the fact that I was designed and fashioned after the creator of this world. I began to affirm with my own mouth repeatedly that I looked like my heavenly father. My life began to change simply because I began to think differently and speak differently towards myself.

When you learn of your true identity, you no longer wish to self-destruct. When you become aware that God made you like Him so that you can fulfill a purpose here on earth, you will begin to view your life differently. You become aware that you are in darkness and you desire to come into God's light. Coming from the darkness into the light is not easy. The devil will try his best to make you stay. He will begin to tempt you with things that pleased you while you lived in darkness, but no matter how many fiery darts he throws at you, you must continue to press towards the light. Being created in the image of God means that you possess the same qualities He has. It means that all of what God is, you are a part of. You will never be as great as God so do not take this created in His image thing out of balance. Just understand God has imparted a small portion of Himself unto you, and because you are divinely connected to Him, you have the power to accomplish God's purpose for you while you are here on earth.

Let us examine the gift of creativity. Just look all around you. Look at all the things you see every day. Everything you see besides the trees, the firmament, the sun, the moon, and the oceans was created by someone's gift of creativity. God has imparted His gift of creativity into our souls and our brains. This means that you possess the ability to be creative. The truth is, when God designed your brain, He made a special place inside your brain that is strictly designed for creativity. God loves it when we are creative. He enjoys seeing that segment of creativity He put in your brain being manifested in this world. He knew that through your creativity, the world would be as it is today. Because God is creative, you too are creative. I hope you are beginning to understand what being created in His image really means. Being created in God's image simply means you have the same characteristics as your father.

God designed you with a mouth just as He has one. Physically, the mouth is the beginning process for digestion of food, but the mouth was designed to hold the most powerful weapon you will ever have, your tongue. In the tongue, there is much power. So much power you can create life or death. That is why God's word tells us so much about the words we speak and how to tame the tongue. It is important for us to learn how to speak the appropriate words that will develop our inner man and create the abundant life of which Christ spoke. Everything that is, God has spoken it to be. The first step to activating that power is to begin to use affirming words. When God spoke the world into its fashion, He had a vision in mind and that vision was all the good that the world has come to be.

Jesus the Affirmer

"I am the bread of life (John 6:35), I am the light of the world (John 8:12), I am the good shepherd (John 10:11), I am the resurrection and the life"(John 11:25).

Let us review the ministry of Jesus. His ministry was all about affirmations of faith. Jesus himself was an affirmer. Did you know that all of His healing miracles were actually affirmed before they took place? If the people did not believe, Jesus' miracle power was limited. Let's examine the healing of the man with leprosy in the book of Matthew (8;2-4). The man plagued with the disease said, "Lord if you are willing, you can make me clean."

Let's study how Jesus responded to the man's affirmation of faith. Jesus reached towards the man and then He said, "I am willing." This statement alone is an affirmation. When Jesus said these magical words, it set the atmosphere for healing to take place.

Next Jesus said, "Be clean!" and immediately the man was clean. When Jesus affirmed the man with leprosy was to be clean, he became clean. Let us examine what has actually taken place.

1. The man with leprosy stated an affirmation of faith: "You can make me clean."

2. When Jesus heard the man's affirmation, He immediately responded, reached out to touch the man, and stated back to him: "I am willing."

3. After Jesus made the statement to the man that He is willing, He affirmed the words, "Be clean." The man immediately became clean. When Jesus affirmed that the man was clean, it happened, and it happened fast.

This story teaches us that every thing must begin with an affirmation of faith, on our behalf, in order to move the heart of Jesus. Something about affirmations allows Jesus to move in our lives.

Let's examine the next miracle, which is one of my favorites. This miracle shows the power in speaking affirmations. This story is the faith of the Centurion (Read Luke 7:7). This man knew that if Jesus only spoke healing into his servant's body, it would be done. He knew that Jesus needed to only speak the word and healing would then take place. The centurion must have heard of the miracles and was moved in his spirit so, that he believed without Jesus actually being there, his servant could still be healed. This man knew of Jesus'greatness, and he knew that if Jesus would just affirm (speak) the words of healing, it would be done. Let's look at what Jesus said. He said, *"I tell you, I have not found such great faith even in Israel"(Luke 7:9)*. Jesus said this because He was amazed this individual actually understood the importance of speaking things aloud in faith. He was amazed that the man understood the importance of speaking a word. Jesus was awed that one person understood the big picture. Jesus was overjoyed that this man knew it was important for him to have enough faith to speak aloud that Jesus needed only to send His word. He understood that Jesus' word was far more important than Him being present in order for the healing to take place. Jesus knew His time on earth would be short lived, and the people would not always have Him in their presence physically.

I believe when He heard of the centurion's faith, He became amazed that someone understood speaking words of faith activates God's power to move on one's behalf. When the people returned home, they found the man well. Scripture does not say Jesus spoke for the man to be made well, nor does it say Jesus laid hands on the man. I personally believe Jesus sent his words of healing and the man became well. Something actually happened without Jesus being there. Something actually happened without Jesus laying a hand on the servant. God's word is living proof we must begin to speak words of faith into our lives. In the present time, Jesus is not here with us physically, however, He waits for his followers (you and I) to begin to speak affirmations of faith. When we speak affirmations of faith, Jesus hears us and begins to move on our behalf in favor with the words of faith spoken.

This is why Jesus said, *"But I tell you that men will have to give account on the Day of Judgment for every careless word they have spoken. For, by your words you will be acquitted, and by your words you will be condemned"(Matthew 12:36).* The words that come out of our mouths play an important role in our lives here on earth and on judgment day as well. When we speak affirmations of faith, God hears us. When we speak words of life, He hears us. When we speak words of death (negative talk), He also hears us. This is why it is imperative that we learn to become positive affirmers of God's promises. We must master the words that come from our mouths. Now let the affirmations begin!

1. A New day

Forget the former things; do not dwell on the past. See I am doing a new thing! Now it springs up; do you not perceive it?

This affirmation is to be spoken each morning. It is intended to help you stay in the present instead of the past. It is also intended to begin your day with a clear conscious and a brand new start. When you lay asleep at night your body begins to replenish itself. Your cells renew themselves while old cells die. Your body repairs tissues so you can be prepared for the next day. Each day you awake, you and the day are made new. You have another chance to make changes in your life, work through some of your issues, and make peace with yourself and others. Yesterday is gone, and you can never have it back, so the things you said and did yesterday are outdated.

I can remember when I first started reaffirming my life, I use to become consumed with all the mistakes I made in the past such as choosing the wrong relationships to be involved in. True, the choices I made led me to the very difficult task of single parenting, but I knew that I could never change the past. I could only face, accept, make peace with my past, move forward with my life, and do my best to raise my girls. I made peace with my yesterdays by taking time to understand and learn the lessons that life was teaching me. Each day I would wake up and affirm, *"Yesterday is gone, and today I am starting all over again."*

As I began to launch out on my journey towards healing and affirming my new life, I messed up every day. I had so many issues and so many dysfunctional habits. I knew I needed to change my behaviors and knew for sure God was the only one who could change me.

I remember having a terrible disorder of my mouth. I kept on cursing. I could not stop. I cussed at people. I cussed while I was driving, and whenever I became angry (which was quite often). I knew my mouth was filthy, and if I were ever going to speak any good into my life, I would have to give up the curse words. I made up in my mind that if I was going to develop an excellent spirit, I had to stop. I remember doing a bible study and learning that God wanted me to rid my mouth of all perverse talk and filthy language. I wanted to live a life that was pleasing to God. I desired to become what I call spiritually beautified, and I knew a godly woman could not possibly become that if she was going around cussing like a sailor all the time. I just had to give it up, but it was very difficult. I would make it through a whole day without cussing, then at the end of the day I would get home, and someone would set me off. I would receive a call from a bill collector, and there I would go cussing them out like a mad woman. Afterwards, I would feel bad because I felt as though I failed. Every day I awoke, I would tell God I was starting back all over again, and I was not going to cuss any more. I told God this at least a thousand times.

I have given up the curse words, because I understand spiritual beauty. True spiritual beauty works continuously to perfect those things in the spirit that are not so perfect, so that the spirit of that individual can begin to reflect the image of God. I knew I would never be perfect, but I felt that it was important at least to strive towards it. I knew that God was not going around speaking curse words to people when He was offended or felt angry towards an individual because of their shortcomings. I realized that there is nothing beautiful about talking filthy. There is nothing cute about horrible name calling to those who are simply doing their jobs and inquiring about money you owe them. It makes no sense to get so angry with people and call them curse words. It only showed how spiritually imbalanced I was, and how I had no self-control over the words I spoke. I came to the realization that when I got frustrated and angry, I began to cuss. I started doing an exercise to help me stop. Whenever I became frustrated, I would say anything but a curse word. Instead of saying the F word, I would say something else that started with the letter F. Doing this exercise and affirming each day that I was not going to cuss eventually helped me to stop.

To this very day, I make a special effort to ensure that my mouth stays clean. I make a special effort not to say words I will regret and have to repent for later. I have become grateful that each day is made new. I became aware that each day God wakes me I am being given a second chance. I realized that each day is new so that meant I was made new. I realized that each day I am alive, God is actually giving me another chance to allow His true purpose for me to come forth. Each day that God makes new is a chance for everything in your life to be new.

Remember that each day you awake, God is saying, *"There is still time left to learn and work your salvation out."* God desires us to embrace every day that we are alive. He desires us to know that today we have a new chance to reaffirm the life He intended for us to have since the beginning of time. Isn't it just beautiful to know that each day that grace is given to you to awake, you are given another chance to begin to blossom as flowers do. You are given another chance to change, as do the seasons. Learn to be glad for each new day. Life would be gloomy if the day never ended. It would be horrible to have to live continuously in the same day for the rest of our lives. I do not know how you feel, but it would drive me crazy. Each day you awake God is saying: *"My child each new day that I speak into existence represents a new beginning for you."*

Speak these refreshing words into your brand new day!

Today is a brand new day, and since the day is made new, I am made new. I welcome new gentle experiences that will draw me closer to God's love. For yesterday is gone and will never be given back. Today, I will try new things that invite love, wisdom, and wealth into my life. I welcome new ideas that put me in alignment with God's purpose for me here on earth. I welcome the gift of peace, which will sustain me through any challenges I am presented with today. I also welcome the warm sweet presence of the Holy Spirit who will guide me through this day by His powerful infinite wisdom. For this is the day the Lord has made; I will be glad and rejoice in it. I will forget the former things; I will not dwell on the past. God is doing a new thing in my life! It is now springing up, and I do perceive it! In Jesus' name, it is done.

2. Affirmation of Truth

And you shall know the truth and the truth shall make you free
(John 8: 32).

The truth is very crucial in the healing process. Without the truth, healing cannot take place. Each day we must speak, live, and walk in the truth. When we accept the truth about our present circumstances and ourselves, we can then begin to make choices and decisions that will help us along the process of healing. Knowing and accepting the truth about ourselves allows us to receive healing. When we walk in the light of truth, we are then made free.

I have discovered if you speak from the depths of your soul what you believe to be true, then you are a free spirit. I have also discovered that when an individual person knows what is the truth within his heart, but he is not able to speak his version of truth, this individual is a slave to bondage and deception. When we come into the realization of truth, we rise to a level of awareness that allows us to see the changes in our lives that need to be made. We also realize that without God's help, it is impossible to make those changes.

I had to face the truth about myself. I was twenty-two years old. I had two children, no husband, and I was three thousand miles away from home. The truth about my situation was that I had to provide for my two babies somehow. The truth was I believed very strongly that God would help me if I met him half way. I knew that He would shed light and truth on the direction I needed to go. And guess what? He did.

I had to face the truth about my addiction to men who were not good for me. What was making me cling to men who I knew were not right for me? The truth was my mother abandoned me at the age of five. My uncles and other family members sexually abused me. I was mentally abused, told that I would only end up on drugs and in a life of prostitution. All of this trauma affected me mentally and emotionally and actually became part of who I was. I clung to the type of men whose behavior lined up with my past. Why? Because it was all I knew. These men made me feel like I felt all of my life: abandoned, rejected, confused, and unloved. It was then when the light clicked on. I never knew what it was like to be loved and accepted; yet, I wanted to feel that. My children's fathers did not love themselves or me, and it took the grace of God to show me that they too were victims of a traumatized past.

I understand now that I did not love myself, but how could I? All throughout my childhood, I developed negative emotions about myself due to the unpleasant actions and words of others. I only recreated what I was feeling on the inside of my soul. I have discovered that so many people, especially Christians, live in denial about their emotional status. I believe it is because, as Christians, we feel we must set up some perfect image of God to look a certain way in the presence of others. No one should be blind to the truth about himself, especially a Christian. God's word tells us that if we confess our faults, we can then be healed, but when we hide them within ourselves, we become emotionally damaged.

As a child of God, you should never be afraid to tell yourself the truth. You should never try to present yourself in a certain way before others while you are being destroyed on the inside. You were bought with a price and that is the blood of Christ as a ransom for your freedom. You have a right to walk in the truth and live in the truth. You have a right to accept the truth about your past failures and with God's help, work through your issues without being judged by anyone. The truth is you are not the only one who has been hurt and unable to face the truth about your past. Many walk around every day saying that they're so blessed when the truth is they feel ill on the inside. This is due to denial. Without God's truth, I would not have realized the deep things inside of myself about my past that were causing me to involve myself in situations that were unhealthy.

No matter what your situation is, I encourage you to affirm the truth in your life every day. Begin to figure out what is the truth about you. Never be afraid of the truth, but always welcome its presence. If you are a gossiper, go ahead, accept this as the truth about you, and begin to get a grip on your mouth with prayer. If you are thief, go ahead and accept it as the truth, then pray for change. If you go around sleeping with different men and women, trying to fill empty voids within yourself, accept this as the truth. Whatever it is about you, make no excuses for your behavior, but only tell yourself the truth. When you tell yourself the truth, something happens. You begin to see your true self and all of the things you wish to change. Often, it is quite painful and difficult to accept the truth about you and your ugly ways. This is when you should depend on God to help you get through. Once your spiritual eyes are opened to the truth, your soul becomes uncomfortable with the things that you are beginning to identify with and you will want to make changes in your life. Just remember to keep on telling the truth no matter how hurtful the truth about you and your circumstances may be. The truth will carry you beyond self deception and will put you on the path towards a life long journey of understanding you and developing an intimate relationship with God.

Speak these words of truth into your life today:

I shall walk, live, and speak the truth. For the truth shall make me free. When I am in denial, I will call on the spirit of truth for He shall make me see all truths about my present circumstances and myself very clearly. Telling myself the truth will help me maintain balance in my life and will allow me to heal. When I tell the truth to others and myself, I am developing my character and will shed light on their lives. The truth allows me to walk in freedom daily. For God's truth is a divine healer for my mind, body, and soul. The truth about me is: I stand in the need of healing mentally, physically, and spiritually. As long as I have the breath of life in my body, I am given the opportunity for growth and change. The truth is that Jesus died so that my soul can walk in freedom and in truth. Now that the truth about me has been told, I am now healed. In Jesus' name it is done.

3. Affirmation of Trust

It is better to trust in the Lord than to put confidence in princes
(Psalms 118:9).

Learning to demonstrate trust towards people and God can be very difficult especially for one who has had his or her trust violated time after time. People may let you down and people may hurt you, but God and His word can be trusted. I have learned through living that we all can trust the process of life. God is the process of life. Just think for a minute. Nature does its thing regardless of our trust issues. Whether you trust or not, the sun rises to give us light each day. The seasons change to bring forth harvests. You must learn to trust God always. You must trust that you will make it through each day and each experience.

Let me ask you. Did you make it through your last experience? At the time, it probably felt as though you would not make it, but you did. You made it because you trusted God. You may not have realized it at the time, but some part of you trusted God and that is how you made it through. You made it because you trusted that God would see you through.

The trials in your life do not come to tear you down, but they come to teach you your lessons, they come to awaken you so you can be aware, they come to mature you, they come to teach you patience, and most of all, they come to teach you to love more. After all you have been through, you are still breathing. Trust in God's word. He promises that He has a plan for your life that would give you a future. You may be one who says, "I trust God, but I do not trust people."

"The Lord says, cursed be the man that trusts in man, and makes flesh his arm, and whose heart departs from the Lord" (Jeremiah 17: 5). It is not good to put your trust in man who is but only flesh. God would not want you to do that and neither do I.

You are going to have to trust people at some point in your life, but you are not required to put your trust in them. You are, however, required to put your trust in God, because in God there is everything you will ever need. People cannot give you everything you could possibly need, but God can. You can expect God to do things for you and trust that He will do them because He promised in His Word that He would supply all of your needs. He promises that He would give you the desires of your heart if we take pleasure in Him. He promises that if you trust in Him and His ways, He would make your path very clear. Unfortunately, many of us are doing the opposite. We are putting our trust in people expecting them to make us feel a certain way and expecting them to live up to high levels of standards, and when they fail us, we are so hurt and angry. It is when we do not put our trust in God confusion takes place. People can only do so much. They can only do the best that their minds know how to do. We can not forever be angry and upset at people when they let us down and hurt us. You have to remember that each person that you come into contact with is also on a spiritual journey towards healing just as you are. Pray for and forgive people when they hurt you, then examine who you are putting your trust in. Is it that person or is it God?

Today is the perfect day to begin to prioritize your levels of trust. You should put all of your trust in God. Only He can meet each and every one of your needs. You can and should trust people, but do not put your trust in them because they are merely flesh and will let you down. Trust that God is working with that individual just as He is working with you. Trust that God knows what is best for your life and the other persons life as well. Are you beginning to see how to balance your trust issues? Your not putting your trust in a person, but you are trusting that God loves that person just as much as He loves you. Trust that God can and will take care of you and that person as well.

Speak these words of trust into your life today!

Today, I am now putting all my trust in God and His promises. Today, I am no longer depending on people, but I am depending on God to meet all of my needs physically, spiritually, mentally, and emotionally. I thank God that all of my needs are met. I trust that all things are working together for my good. I trust that I can handle whatever experience is designed to teach me to master my trust in God. Today, I trust that God is God and He knows what is best for me. In Jesus' name, it is done.

4. Affirmation of God's Greatness

Greater is He that is in you, than he that is in the world (1 John 4:4).

There is a measure of greatness that exists within all of us. Because we are created in the image of God and because His spirit lives in us, we are able to accomplish great things. While you were being knitted together in your mother's womb, greatness was being etched into your soul. Each gift we have has been deposited in our souls before we were born. The gifts that were imparted to you were given to you to share in the great responsibility of making this world a better place.

You were given an assignment to complete here on earth, and you were destined for greatness the moment God thought of you. God knew each one of us before He even formed us. He had a plan in mind for you before He brought you into existence. He shared His greatness with you, which is the breath of life. When He breathed into your nostrils, He unselfishly shared His intelligence, His power, His creativity, and every great thing that is in Him with you. Each breath that you take, you are actually divinely connected with all that God is. All the beauty that God deposited inside of you is known as His greatness. This greatness must be brought forth, but it first must be activated.

The first step towards activating your greatness is to simply realize and accept that it exists inside of you. You may have a nice house, a brand new car, and a great salary, but none of these things make you great. Greatness has always existed in you simply because

God lives within you. What makes you great? God makes you great. Believing you are great because God lives in you and using all of the precious gifts that He has equipped you with makes you even greater. Withdrawing the talents that God has blessed you with and exercising them here on earth, leads you into greatness and gives honor and glory to Him. Here we have a chain reaction: God lives in you and that makes you great, and because He lives within you, you will accomplish great things, which can only lead you into greatness. All those wonderful talents you have been blessed with that you have been sitting on all of your life, is known as God's greatness. You probably have settled for the lesser things in life because you did not understand that God's greatness lives inside of you. God's greatness will continue to live inside of you as long as you are breathing and will be with you when you enter into eternal life.

I always knew I had several talents. I loved singing, writing, and studying the miracles of science. Would I become a famous recording star? Would I become a doctor? Would I write books and become a famous author? I ran myself crazy trying to make a decision on what to do with my life. One day, I just made up in my mind that I would use all three of my talents and what ever I ended up doing, would be exactly what God created me to do. I decided to do a little singing, writing, and attend medical school. I figured, what heck, if I cannot make up my mind, I would just be a singing author who would one day heal the lives of many. And that is just what I did. One night, I dreamed I was singing, so the next day I wrote a song and named it "Something Better." A friend of mine from school gave me some music that matched it perfectly. I then recorded my very first song. I had it copy written, and I was happy. It did not matter if I became a famous star. All that mattered to me was that I shine before the eyes of my creator, because I was using my gift of writing and singing instead of just letting it go to waste.

I wrote other songs when I had the time. I was busy studying for my biology or chemistry classes and taking care of Jasmine and Nia Somehow, it all worked out. I discovered my talents and began to use them.

I have had an exciting adventure discovering what my talents are and actually using them to glorify God. Making an effort to actually bring forth my talents, taught me to believe in myself and has taught me just how great I really am. Not in the eyes of man, but in the eyes of my creator. I realize that God considers me great because I was actually expressing the part of Him that lives within me by using what He gave me.

It is God's desire for you to discover His greatness inside of you, activate His greatness inside of you, and bring it forth. Whatever talents you have been blessed with, go ahead and begin to exercise them. Do not be concerned with what others think of you and your marvelous ideas. Only be concerned about what God thinks of you. I can guarantee that God will smile on you when He begins to notice that you have finally made the decision to bring forth the great things He has deposited in you. Remember there is no failure in God. Whenever I feel discouraged or feel like I have failed, I tell God, "Well, at least if I meet you today, I can stand before you and declare that I used what you gave me to the best of my ability and I did try to do all that you told me to do."

With that, I am satisfied. Speak to the great spirit of God within you, and He will surely come out! He will manifest Himself in your life. You will begin to use the gifts He has given to you for his glory. You will begin to think and speak differently. You will begin to accomplish things that you never thought you could accomplish. Go ahead and discover your God given greatness.

Call forth the greatness of God from inside of you:

Now that I realize why I exist, I shall accomplish that purpose. Now that I understand the divine power that is within me, I shall activate it. Now that I understand the gifts that were imparted unto me, I shall use them. Greater is He that is in me than he that is in the world. Now that I understand that the kingdom of God exists within me, through my good thoughts, through my good deeds, through my love, through my patience, through my dreams, through my hopes, I can now manifest its greatness by bringing these treasures into the universe. I speak to the greatness of God within me. Come forth by the power of the Holy Spirit. I speak to the great ideas that I have always hid within my heart because of fear. Spring forth great ideas and manifest yourself through my mind and the power of my words so I can bring all of this greatness within myself into existence. In Jesus' name, it is done.

5. Affirmation of Courage

Arise; for this matter belongs unto thee: we also will be with thee: be of good courage, and do it (Ezra 10:4).

In order to live a life filled with faith, we must learn to develop courage. My definition of courage is to speak the truth, to live the truth, to walk in the light of truth, and to be fearless. If you believe something to be true live it, walk it, speak it, be it, and most of all, pursue it. Courage will allow you to do what is in your heart!

I was eighteen years old and all grown up. What was I going to do with my life? I had no children, no ties to anyone, and no major responsibilities. My aunt always encouraged me to move to Atlanta. She thought it would be best for me to move far away from my family because I had suffered so much abuse. I was afraid to move all the way from San Francisco to Atlanta. Where would I live? How would I take care of myself? Was I ready to step out into the real world, far away from all my family and friends? Would someone take advantage of me? After all, I was only eighteen years old.

It was July of 1994. I worked at Kentucky Fried Chicken, and I remember thinking to myself while working one day, *There has got to be something better out there for me. I am moving to Atlanta as soon as I get paid.* While I waited for payday, I prayed and asked God if it was okay for me to go to Atlanta.

I actually remember this still voice within myself saying, *Wherever you go, I will be with you. If you stay here, I am with you. If you move to Georgia, I am with you.*

After hearing those words, I decided I would go to Atlanta. I figured if God was going to be with me everywhere that I went, I should at least try to make it on my own. Payday came and I purchased a one-way ticket to Atlanta, Georgia. I then went home to pack all my belongings, which totaled to a couple of duffle bags stuffed with clothes, makeup, hair supplies, personal care products, and my bible. I put all my bags at the front door and anxiously waited for my dad to get home so he could take me to the bus station. The hardest thing for me to do was to actually tell my daddy that I was leaving on such a short notice. I did not feel I should discuss my decision with him before making it, because I did not want him or any of my family to try to convince me to stay. When he came home and saw my bags at the door, he asked me where did I think I was going. I said, "Daddy, I am moving to Atlanta. I need a change."

He asked me questions like where was I going to live. I told him I was going to stay with my cousin Dwayne who was in college in Atlanta at the time. I was glad to have at least one relative down there so I would not be totally all alone. My dad did not think it was a good idea, but he and I both knew that I was an adult, and the decision was mine to make. He took me to the bus station, and I rode the bus for two days and sixteen hours.

On my journey to Atlanta, the bus stopped many places for rest and food breaks. I felt like I was on an adventure. I was excited and could hardly wait to arrive to my new home. I actually felt like there was purpose in me coming to Atlanta. I wanted to sing and make records at the time, and I believed I would do so. I arrived in Atlanta with about two hundred dollars in my pocket. As soon as I got off the bus, my cousin and his best friend were there to greet me. The first words that came out of his mouth were, "Your daddy called and asked me to keep a close eye on you. He also told me to look out for you."

I know that I hurt my dad by just up and leaving, and I knew that he was going to worry, but I wanted to live my life. I became employed again at Kentucky Fried Chicken a couple of days after I arrived. Money was tight and payday was two weeks away. I was down to my last few dollars and I needed money. I was not the type to sleep around with guys for money and I could have, but instead I said a prayer to the Lord. I remember asking Him to please provide me with enough money to last me until payday. I also remembered the comforting words that He spoke to my spirit before I left stating that He would be with me.

Later on, that afternoon, a young gentleman and I decided to go to the store, and as we were leaving, I stepped on something. When I looked down, I noticed that it was a wallet. I picked it up, and there was over three hundred dollars inside. My face lit up. My heart was overjoyed. The Lord had heard my prayer. I was not actually in a committed relationship to God at the time. I just knew to say a prayer when I needed Him, so I did not think twice about trying to find out to whom the money belonged. All I knew is I prayed that morning, having very little money in my pocket, and that afternoon I had over three hundred dollars in my hands. I always believed in sharing and my friend who I was with was a student at Morehouse College and was struggling himself. I gave him some, and we enjoyed the rest of our day. From that day on, I knew some unseen force was looking out for me, and I knew what God spoke to me was true. He would be with me wherever I went.

When we step out and begin to do things we have never done before, we are exercising courage. I believed that I would be happy in Atlanta and that God would watch over me. Believing this was exercising my faith. I then worked up the courage to leave everything behind, including my sister and my brother who I loved dearly. All of us grew up together. What would life be like without my sister? You can believe something all you want, but I have learned through this experience and several others that if you do not have the courage to do what you believe in, then you will never see what you believe come to pass. It is detrimental that you learn how to develop a courageous spirit.

Our heroes of the bible were no wimpy guys. They were bold and courageous. David did not kill the giant by running and hiding. I like to believe David exercised his faith by simply making up in his mind that he would be the one to slay this humongous giant and receive the reward. He believed this to be true. Then, he worked up some courage in his heart, and with a slingshot and a stone, he killed the giant and cut off his head.

If you study this story very carefully, you will notice that right before he killed Goliath, he spoke nothing but affirmations. He spoke the "I will affirmation" (1 Samuel 17; 45) Here is what David told the giant: *"You come against me with sword, spear, and javelin, but I come against you in the name of the Lord Almighty, the God of the armies of Israel, whom you have defied. This day the Lord will hand you over to me, and I will strike you down and cut off your head. Today I will give the carcasses of the Philistine army to the birds of the air and the beasts of the earths, and the whole world will know that there is a God in Israel. All those gathered here will know that it is not by sphere or sword that the Lord saves; for the battle is the Lord's, and He will give all of you into our hands."* While David spoke this powerful affirmation aloud to the Giant, I believe adrenalin was pumping throughout his body and the spirit of courage aroused in him and he did just what he affirmed.

In order to live your dreams, faith is the key to believing that they will come true, yet you must allow the spirit of courage to rise up in you in order to operate your faith in making your dreams come true. When the spirit of courage rises in you, it does one thing. It abolishes fear. With courage, fear cannot exist. Have you ever wanted to say something to someone, but you could not find the courage to do so? I know I have. The reason you could not say what you needed to say was that fear gripped you. Because you feared, you could not say what was in your heart. You failed to say the words that needed to be said. This may have caused you to miss some very valuable opportunities. The very next time you want to express yourself, but you cannot because of fear, call forth for the spirit of courage to rise up in you and speak what is in your heart. Just remember to say what you need to say in the spirit of love. Whatever it is you have always wanted to do, just do it. Begin to speak these words of courage in your life every day from this day on and watch how your life begins to change. I guarantee that you will begin to say things that are in your heart and do the things that you have never had the courage to do!

Speak these words of courage into your life today.

I have the courage to face life and its daily challenges. I have the courage to press on in spite of all of the obstacles that are before me. Thank you great and mighty God for courage. You said to be courageous. So I will. I am becoming fearless. Therefore, I am becoming courageous. With fear, I can accomplish nothing, but with courage I will accomplish the impossible. I am living my dreams because of courage. I am fulfilling my purpose because of courage. I can speak the truth in love because of courage. I can look fear in its face and say, "Get thee behind me!" because of courage. From this day on, I will be courageous. Thank you God for infusing me with the gift of courage. I am not afraid, but I am courageous. In Jesus' name it is done.

6. Affirmation of Confidence

Beloved, if our heart condemn us not, then we have confidence towards God (1 John 3: 21).

In order to achieve our highest good, I believe God wants all of His children to obtain something I call God confidence. Without the confidence that comes from God, we will not live a life of faith and we will not do the things God called us to do. Without confidence, we will become smothered in fear, therefore, inhibiting our spiritual growth. When you lack confidence, you feel inferior to others, you may even feel envious at times, and you feel as though you do not have what it takes to get what your heart desires. When you do not believe the best about yourself, you become paralyzed and afraid. You may have God-inspired ideas, but because you lack confidence, you believe your ideas are not good enough. You then convince yourself of that, and therefore, you don't make your ideas come true.

God confidence is the kind of confidence God infuses you with when He assigns you a specific assignment as you develop a personal relationship with him. God confidence will give you the power to manifest all your hopes and dreams to fulfill His plan for your life. Study God's word and you will begin to read about all of His prophets. You will notice all of His servants were filled with confidence. Most of our bible heroes did not start off having confidence, but when God finished speaking His word to them, they went forward in awesome confidence. When God called Moses from the burning bush, Moses was terrified. He did not have enough confidence in himself to go before the Pharaoh and declare in the name of the God of Jacob, to let the Hebrew people go. God began to reveal Himself to Moses little by little. Each time God showed himself to Moses, I believe he was infused with more and more confidence. Each time God plagued the land of Egypt, Moses became filled with more confidence in God. God confidence gave Moses the courage to keep on going to the Pharaoh, insisting the Hebrew slaves be set free. Moses was filled with confidence because He had a personal encounter with God. If Moses did not have special encounters with God, I know he would not have had the courage to stand so boldly before Pharaoh and say, "Let my people go!"

Martin Luther King was also filled with God confidence. God empowered him to stand before a racist nation and demand equal rights for African American people. God filled him with so much confidence that he was willing to stand for what was right even if it cost him his life. When God gives a person a vision, He also fills him with confidence to go forward with the dream put in his heart. God will give all of His children different experiences to teach them confidence.

At one time, I had no confidence in myself at all. I did not believe in myself. I did not think I could do anything right, but God taught me how to have confidence in a very special way. I am a single parent, and I had trouble believing God could send a decent man into my life because I have children. I used to think no one decent would desire me because he would not want to be bothered with my children. I know now that this was of the enemy. It was his tactic to trick me into believing this lie he put in my mind because I had children, I would have to settle for what I had always settled for–trash. At that time in my life, I did not know what it meant to have faith. I wanted to have faith, but I just did not know how to believe in myself or God's awesome power.

I remember asking God to give me a faith experience that would teach me how to have faith to believe that He had greater things in store for me. I had no idea that in order for me to have faith, I needed confidence to back me up. Boy did God answer this prayer. He not only taught me what it means to have faith, but He taught me to

48

become a confident young woman who believes in herself and the desires of her heart.

Shortly after I started working at the hospital, I happened to run into a young man that instantly quickened my spirit. This young man was not only handsome but was also a brilliant surgeon. There were many issues inside of me from my past that had to be healed, and I believe God allowed me to have this experience with this man to teach me what faith is, how confidence must go along with it, and also to heal my wounded heart. I had not actually met this man yet, but the first time we saw each other I felt as though I knew him somehow. That evening when I went home, I wondered who he was. I mean, my soul actually felt as though we met before, but I knew we had not.

At that time in my life, I was praying for God to send me a husband and a good one at that. I believe every woman has prayed this prayer before, and I believe many women at some point in their lives have believed that a certain man was going to be their husband. I would meet different men who were interested in me, but I had to ask God first. Somehow, God would show me this person was not in my best interest. I promised God after I was left with another child to raise alone, I would listen when He warned me of potential danger. I met different men who wanted to date me that year, but each time I prayed about them, God would say no. I had to learn to listen because Lord knows I did not want any more drama. So, I just gave up.

I decided to pray just one more prayer. I asked God if the young gentleman that I came across that day was my husband. I said, "Lord, if this man is the husband that you've chosen for me, please let the phone ring within the next five minutes (be careful what you ask for)." It was about one in the morning. No one usually called my house that late at night, but it rang that night, and boy, was I happy. Boy, was I excited! After all the no's, I finally got a yes! I had finally met my husband (at least this is what I thought). Several months went by and I did not see him again. I began to pray every day that one day we would have the chance to meet. After praying several prayers, he and I finally met. We met in a very strange way. I would always have dinner in the café at the hospital where I worked. I had a friend who worked there as a cashier and she knew him. I grew tired of praying. I asked her to tell him when she saw him, that someone wanted to meet him. She agreed to do so and inform him of the time that I would be in the café. The very next evening, I was eating, and he actually came into the café. I was so happy. My friend told him that someone wanted to meet him and he was actually coming to find out who it was. As he walked by to go towards the phone to make a call, I waved at him while smiling from ear to ear. I actually believed he was looking for me. I thought he was using the phone just to be using it. I thought my friend saw him and told him about me and he had come to meet me. As I waved, he approached me and we introduced ourselves. I discovered he was sort of a jerk. He was too cocky, but I did not care. I finally had my prayer answered.

The next time I saw my friend in the café, I thanked her for telling him. Surprisingly, she said she did not get the chance to tell him that at all. She said she was at home sick with the flu. I did not know what to think. Instantly, I remember hearing these words in my spirit.

You see Melissa, I do not need your assistance in trying to make things happen. Divine timing is on your side. Allow me to make things happen . I do not need your help.

I wish my heart, soul, and mind would have listened and trusted that voice because it was the voice of the Holy Spirit.

After we met the first time, it was several months before we met again. I had almost given up. So one night, before I went to bed, I decided to pray again. I said, "Lord, I am getting frustrated, and I am starting to believe the phone ringing in the middle of the night was a coincidence. I can't keep believing something that is not true, so if this man is my husband, please let me see him tomorrow. Please let him start a conversation with me, and then, I will know for sure he is the one, and I will not bother you anymore. Please do this for your servant."

Now I had not seen him in about three months, but the next day after I said that prayer, I went to get coffee from the cafeteria when

I accidentally pulled a breakfast tray. I put the tray back on the shelf, and when I turned around, he was standing right behind me. My spirit jumped, and I had to get a hold of myself.

He said, "Hello, long time no see."

Trying to play it cool, I said hesitantly, "Hello."

He actually started a conversation with me, asking where I was from. I was so happy all over, I could have screamed, but I did not. I told him I was from San Francisco, and he asked what was I doing so far away from home. I explained that I was in college. As we talked, I asked him where he was from, and he pointed up to the sky and said, "Heaven," and turned around very quickly to grab a piece of fruit or something from the breakfast bar.

Startled, I said, "Excuse me, where did you say you were from?"

He said again, "I said heaven."

At this point, I became startled. I could not believe it. I thought to myself, *Was this young man a fly on the wall last night while I was praying, or did God really hear me while I prayed?* Quickly snapping out of my own thoughts, I said aloud laughing, "Oh, me too."

From that point on, I was convinced he was the one that God had chosen for me.

We became acquainted, and we talked from time to time. Somehow, I had to work up the confidence to tell him that I only met him because I prayed every day and believed I would. How would I work up the nerve to tell him I thought he was the one for me? Would he believe me if I shared this information with him? Would he think I was nuts? It took some months, but I finally told him. He actually believed me. I told him my story and how I prayed and seemed to have gotten answers, and he was tickled. I remember one day he told me that he loved all of the confidence that was inside of me. Little did he know God was using him to help me develop confidence within myself that I never had. I did not tell him that I was struggling with confidence issues. I just let him believe that I was the most confident young lady that he would ever meet. I do not think he had a clue it was the first time in my life I was able to have enough confidence to actually say what I believed to be true in my heart.

As we got to know each other, I discovered that he was very self-centered but very sensitive and kind. He discovered that I was anxious and bossy but the most beautifully spirited woman he had ever come across. I wanted us to be together right then. I was inconsiderate because I did not consider his residency at the hospital, trying to fulfill his life long dream of being a surgeon. He did not actually have time for a relationship, but I kept on. I would call him, and he was always at the hospital. I began to think he was not interested in me until one morning I ran into him in the cafeteria and he asked me if I wanted to sit down and have breakfast with him.

As we ate breakfast, he explained to me that each time he would see me things became difficult for him. I believe he was trying to tell me he liked me, but I was a distraction for him. I new deep in my heart that this young man liked me a lot, but he did not have time for what I wanted and felt that I was ready for at the time.

One Easter Sunday, he and I were having a conversation, and I became frustrated with him. I remember telling him that if he did not believe in me, then he should look me in my eyes and tell me so. I told him that if he could tell me that he did not, I would walk away and never bother him again. He stopped and stared me right in my eyes and said very seriously, "I believe you, Melissa."

My heart almost stopped and I felt as though I was melting. Here I was telling this handsome intelligent surgeon that he was my husband and he actually believed me. When he said that, I looked at him with a puzzled look on my face and said, "You do?"

As the years passed by, it seemed as if we would never be together, and I became very impatient. He started to grow tired of me pressuring him and acting dysfunctional, and I became tired of waiting and dealing with his cocky attitude. One night, I asked him did he ever pray and ask God if I was the woman for him? He said, "Yes, I did."

I said, "Well, what did God say?"

He said, "I prayed and asked God to send someone into my life, and then, you came." Then, he became angry and screamed at me,

"Why are you doing this to me?"

I simply said, "I do not know. I just want us to be together now." I became angry while he was yelling at me. He then explained that he was unsure of what happened between us and said he needed me to understand the concept of God's timing. I did not have a clue back then about the concept of God's timing. I did not want to hear about God's timing back then. All I knew is that I met my husband and I was ready to jump over the broom stick!

We stopped speaking to each other after that, and I was deeply hurt. For a whole year, we did not speak. A few times when I tried to call him, he would call right back, and when I picked up the phone, he would slam it in my face. Sometimes, I wouldn't even have called him, and he still called and hung up the phone in my face. I do not know why he would call and hang up in my face for no apparent reason. I did not know why we were both acting so crazy. I had no clue that somehow God was trying to heal our souls of some sort of spiritual dysfunction. We all must live and learn our lessons, and boy, did I learn.

This gentleman had some good qualities as well. He never tried to take advantage of me and get me into bed. I thank God I was being protected by divine intervention. He knew I was a single mom, and he explained that his mom raised him alone. I think because of that he kept his cool, and I am so glad he did. Another good quality was his patience with me, because there were times I did compulsive things and he overlooked them. He always seemed very concerned about my feelings and that I was doing okay.

Today, I cannot say he is my God-ordained husband, but I can say God did design us to meet and learn things about each other and ourselves. I am glad to have met him, and I think it is beautiful that he took the time to listen to me and my divine experiences.

I remember reading in a book written by Michelle McKinney Hammond who said that right before our real mate shows up, there is usually one experience that actually prepares us.

This whole experience taught me about the importance of patience, how to believe in myself, and how to pray until something happens. This man played a very important role in my life, in the area of confidence, and because of my experience with him, confidence still resides with in me.

Meeting different people and having experiences with them, is an avenue I believe God uses to teach life lessons. Most of the lessons we learn in life are through experiences with other people. Most of the trials and tribulations that are presented to us usually involve other people. We learn from other people. We need one another to live, learn, heal, grow, and help master our lessons in life. Just because he and I did not end up married to one another, did not mean that life was over. I enjoyed that experience. I extracted the lessons and moved on.

I believe God allowed our souls to cross each other's paths so that we could somehow help one another heal on a spiritual level and also to prepare both of us for near future events in our lives. I have moved on with my life, and I am sure he has as well. I often pray that each one of his surgeries is successful and all is well with him. I know now that it is very important to practice patience with people and it is very important to allow divine timing to unfold in my life. I also learned God has a specific time for everything, and if you try to move ahead of the plan, you only make matters worse. I know now that it is very important to treat people with love and respect because you do not know who God will put in your pathway to teach you different lessons about yourself such as: confidence, patience, and most of all, love.

God wants to build your confidence in Him so you will go forward and do great work! God will build your confidence through the power of His word. God will build your confidence through a personal encounter with Him. God will bring different experiences into your life to teach you confidence. Embrace them and be of good courage. The lesson will never be more than you can bear, but it will be one that is fitting just for you! Always remember to embrace your experiences, because it is during these situations that God will teach you more and more about Himself. God will infuse you with confidence every day as you seek Him. Focus in on His promises, and welcome each experience designed to help you develop God confidence. You will begin to find yourself gaining more and more confidence every single day. Here is an affirmation that will help you to a new beginning toward a life filled with confidence.

Speak these words of confidence into your life today!

Today, I am going to believe in myself. Tomorrow, I am going to believe in myself. Every day, I am going to believe in myself. For God so believed in me and loved me, He gave His Son as a ransom for my sake. Therefore, I am equipped with God confidence. I am doing all that my creator desires for me to do. I am living, learning, teaching, loving, growing, glowing, and going with the flow of life in the full confidence of God. I am now bringing forth my God given ideas in full confidence. I am confident God's word is true. I am confident all of His promises for my life are happening even now as I am speaking. I am confident in my dreams. I am confident in my prayers. I am confident in my God-given purpose, which is to live a life filled with faith love and hope. I am confident in this: All things do work together for the good of those who love the Lord and who are called according to His purpose. I am confident that I shall have my heart's desires because my heart's desires are desires that bring glory to God and healing to others. I am confident that my face, my shape, my hair, my skin color, my eyes, my hands, my feet, and my whole being are a true representation of God my creator. So therefore, I will hold steadfast to the truth about myself with full confidence that I am and the great I am has made me good! In Jesus'name, it is done.

7. Affirmation of Light

But you are a chosen generation, a royal priesthood, a holy nation, His own special people, that you may proclaim the praises of Him who called you out of darkness into His marvelous light (1 Peter 2:9).

When people become infused with the light of God, they then become aware of their true selves. They begin to see things more clearly. Their purpose and assignments here on earth are made known to them. Things that were once dim become bright. The light of God is what I call a spiritual revelation. I believe this is why the bible speaks of it frequently. The light of God will make people know the truth about themselves. When people are blind to the truth about themselves, they know not the things of God. They are living in spiritual darkness. Spiritual darkness includes deception of one's higher self, lack of knowledge and wisdom pertaining to the things of God, and deep feelings of uncertainty of one's choices and decisions. People living in spiritual darkness may be ones who walk this earth feeling lost. The light of God introduces them to their highest capabilities. They then become more knowledgeable to the things of the spirit (God), and they become more confident in their decision-making process. When people receive the light of God, they accept the truth about God and themselves. They accept that the way to God is through the Son, and through the Son, they receive the light that will lead them to everlasting life.

I once walked in spiritual darkness. I could not, would not, and did not know how to walk in the light of God. My emotions and my mind were so damaged from my past abuse that I accepted my dysfunctional behaviors as normal because they were all I knew. Subconsciously, I surrounded myself with everything that was familiar to me: rejection, emotional abuse, and unloving relationships. I connected with people who would make me feel as I felt as a child–unloved. At the time, I did not know I was connecting with the wrong type of people to recreate a feeling so that I would feel like I had always felt. When I experienced the light of God, I realized I was in darkness. I remember telling myself repeatedly that I had to do something about my issues. I prayed and asked God to help me disconnect from my past. I cried out to the Lord many nights to deliver me from my behaviors. With time, I did get better, and I slowly realized I had to separate myself from every relationship I was involved in that made me feel abused, rejected, and unloved. I had to end quite a few friendships, and I definitely had to execute my unhealthy relationships with men. It took a lot of time, and today I am still working at it.

Satan will do whatever it takes to keep you in darkness. He will keep on putting bad people in your pathway that are also in darkness to either keep you in a spiritual state of darkness or to pull you from God's light back into darkness. God allows this to happen because He wants to develop your skills to assure your soul is being healed and made whole. God wants you to recognize darkness from a mile away, because once you recognize it, you can begin to shun it. In other words you'll be able to smell a no good snake when it presents itself to you disguised in love and friendship. You will not have to be deceived as Adam and Eve were.

I would like to share an experience I had of God's light while I was asleep one night. I can best describe His light as a magnetic force that draws the spirit of a human being towards a level of closeness with Himself. His light is warm, and it shines very, very bright. Once I saw His light, it was not something unfamiliar to me. Somehow, my spirit was very familiar with it. Once this light connected to my spirit, there was no resisting it. It was simply irresistible. As I lay asleep, I dreamt, I was standing outside and the sky began to open up.

Something that resembled a ball was thrown down out of the sky towards me. I recall letting the ball fall to the ground. I then reached down to pick it up. I looked towards the sky, which was opened, and saw a gleaming light that shone brighter than the sun itself. My spirit was instantly drawn towards this light. Its warmth felt so comforting, and I knew my spirit wanted to remain with this light forever.

My spirit began to go toward this light because I saw a big hole in the sky that looked as though it was closing. I remember thinking, *I must get to the top before the hole closes up.* My soul felt very warm and totally at peace while I traveled through the presence of light. As I reached what I call the top of the sky and looked through the hole, I then saw what resembled a long passageway sort of like a tunnel. I looked through and I decided I wanted to go. I did not care about anything that I left behind at that moment. All I knew was I desired to remain in the presence of this light always. I remember a spiritual being standing at the hole. Its back was turned on me. I was not able to see its face. I only glimpsed the back of its white robe. I saw that He was wearing sandals.

As the being stood guarding the hole, I pleaded with it to allow me to go with it, but it said to me, "It is not your time." It then went through the passageway and the hole sealed all the way shut.

As the passageway closed, my heart grew sad. I actually went back down to the ground. My spirit grew sad. I held the ball in my hands and then I awoke out of my sleep. I was puzzled because I did not know what the ball actually represented. After that encounter, I began to write and my life was changing very quickly. I began to see all things in the light. I would study my bible and things became so clear to me.

After this encounter, when I lay asleep, often I would actually hear heavenly beings speaking to me about God. They would share things with me. I would then awake and record them in my journal. The heavenly beings would also minister to me through melody. They would show me myself singing and the very next day when I would awake, the words and the melody were in my head. I would then write the words I heard while I lay asleep and create a song.

Sometimes these beings would sing to me melodies from heaven.

One night as I lay asleep, I saw a gate that was made of solid pearls. It was very beautiful. It was pure white and every thing on the gate was made of pearls. The top of the gate had two huge balls that were made of pearls. The vision was so beautiful, I could not take my eyes off of it.

As I gazed into its beauty, I heard angels singing, "Come and see the glory of your God." They sang this so beautifully over and over again. My behavior towards others and myself began to change. I believe God gave me a special gift from heaven, and He sent an angel to deliver it to me. I believe the angel of God gave me what God wanted me to have, but it was also his or her responsibility to ensure that I did not go through that passageway. I know that if I went through the passageway, I would have actually died in my sleep. This experience was one I will never forget. God gave me something special, and He foresaw that my soul received it, yet I was protected from passing into the afterlife.

This experience allows me to bear witness that the light of God is real and its gazing beauty is a magnetic welcoming force that heals our soul. God's light is a light of healing. Welcoming the presence of light into your life and any of your circumstances will reveal the truth of who you actually are and the healing your spirit desires. I know without a doubt that if you call forth the light of God it will shine through you as bright as a star. Let this light fill you up so it will pour forth from you, allowing you to change your life and the lives of others you meet. Allow it to bring forth the healing and truth your soul longs for. Always remember, Jesus is that light!

Call forth on the light of the most high God into your life.

I call forth the light of God. The light of God is now filling every part of my being. I am now filled with light. I welcome the warm presence of light. This light is now warming my inner self. I am receiving the healing light of God. Let there be light within me. Now there is light. Light is now shining through every dark circumstance in my life, so that the truth is being brought forth now. There is no confusion with light. The light is now bringing me out of darkness. My mind is being filled with your truth oh great light. My heart is being filled with your truth and radiance oh great light. My entire body is being illuminated with your glorious magnetic force of great light. The light of God now shines through me so bright I am a healing vessel to others. Thank you great God for infusing me with your light. In Jesus' name, it is done.

8. Affirmation of Peace

Peace I leave you, my peace I give unto you: not as the world ***gives****, give I unto you. Let not your heart be troubled, neither let it be afraid* (John 14:27).

The gift of peace is a blessing from God. We must face all the trials and tribulations we go through each day in order to achieve this gift. Life is full of many obstacles and problems each day. Jesus was fully aware of what we would have to go through, and He has been gracious enough to leave us some survival tools. He left us the promise of the Holy Spirit, the truth (His word), and the gift of peace. When the spirit of a person cannot experience peace, it suffers a great deal of restlessness and anxiety. Where there is no peace, people become so overwhelmed in their minds and their souls that they have a nervous breakdown and have to spend time in the mental institution. It is quite sad that people have to end their own lives because they feel as though they have no hope or peace of mind. When a person's spirit is troubled, there can be no peace. This is why Jesus warned us to not allow our hearts to be troubled. He did not say we would be trouble free, but He did not want us to be so consumed with the troubles of this life to the point where we have no peace of mind.

Peace should reside in people's soul and mind. When people receive the gift of peace, they are able to go through all of their tests, trials, and experiences knowing God is with them every minute and every second of the hour. When people are not at peace, they often doubt and wonder if God is present or if God left them to suffer. They often feel restless and anxious. I am sure there have been times when you and I have both wondered if God abandoned us, or if He was punishing us for something we did in our past. When these times fall upon us, we need to pray and ask God to anoint us with the gift of peace. We need to pray about everything we are feeling. We need to pray and tell God all of our troubles even if the problem is very private. We need to build a continuous life of prayer. God's word promises us through prayer we can receive peace that will guard our hearts and minds. We need to begin to lose ourselves in God's word and allow our spirits to be comforted while we are going through trials and tests. We also need to pray until peace overwhelms our spirit, even if it means we have to pray on through the night.

We must learn to take advantage of God's gift of peace through Jesus Christ. Why? Because Jesus died so you may have life and have it more abundantly. He died so you could be set free. He gave His life so you could have peace knowing that in Him you shall inherit eternal life. Would you like to know who really has no peace? The enemy. His mind is never at peace. It is of no surprise to me. He goes around keeping up so much chaos and he is constantly trying to use others as vessels of chaos to keep up wickedness and confusion. I doubt he could ever be at peace. I know I could never be at peace if I was on my way to everlasting damnation. Do not let the enemy steal your peace from you. Do what is necessary to maintain a life filled with peace. It may mean separating from those who cause strife, chaos, and confusion in your life, but do what it is you have to do to create a peaceful environment around you and your home.

Years ago, I was living in a housing project in Fourth War, Atlanta. My youngest daughter Nia was just born and times were quite difficult. Nia's father did not want to have anything to do with her or me, and his actions towards us caused me a lot of grief. For the first six weeks of her life, he denied paternity, and there is no hurt like having the man you have shared yourself with on an intimate level deny he is the father of your child. I felt so ashamed. Every day, I told myself how stupid I was to be left to raise another child alone. I cried every day, and my mind was never at peace due to the heavy responsibilities of being a single mother.

The only place I could find peace was in the presence of God. I attended church services regularly. Going to church somehow saved me from totally shutting down and going into a deep depression. To add to my sorrows, my best friend was killed in a car accident, and I never got the chance to say goodbye. In fact, our last time seeing each other was not a very pleasant farewell. His death sunk me to a very low point in my life. For some time, I blamed myself for his death. I had no peace. I was angry and frustrated with my chaotic life. I lay down on my bed and I cried so many tears I could actually feel them pouring from my face into my hands. I was so weary and so afraid. I could not understand why was I a target for pain. Why did I always end up feeling hurt? I remember asking Jesus to please come and give me some peace because I really needed it.

As I slept that night, I dreamt I was in a place. A place that was not here on earth. It resembled earth yet it was not. I remember seeing trees, grass, and roads. I felt like this place had a different atmosphere and the colors of the things that I saw were so much brighter than here on earth. I remember seeing this being stretching out its hand towards me as if it was saying come. This being's face was white like pure snow. Its hair was also white and resembled that of a sheep. The being also wore a long white robe. I precisely remember what looked like golden sashes being embedded in the robe. Its eyes had a glossy glaze in them and resembled charcoal. I was frightened. For I had never laid eyes on anything of this nature before.

Several others followed this being as if they were in a line. As the being signaled for me to come, I began to run out of fear. As I was running, I looked behind me to see if it was close behind, and I saw it draw its right hand back and throw something towards me. Whatever it threw from its hand hit my back and filled my whole spirit with beautiful vibes. It kind of felt like you might feel if you get goose bumps, but this feeling was so powerful that I felt it all over my entire body. I began to smile and run with gladness in my heart. I remember running and running, and I felt great joy.

I did not remember the dream until I was driving to work the next day, and I asked God for peace. Immediately, the whole dream replayed itself in my mind, and I knew someone from the heavenly realms came and gave me what I asked for–peace. At that very moment while driving to work, my spirit and my mind knew everything would be fine. I begin to cry and praise God on my way to work. I tried to figure out who the being was. For quite sometime, I just assumed it was my great grandmother who passed away.

Some months later, I was browsing through the book of Revelations (Rev. 1;12-18), and John was describing this heavenly being, which he perceived as the son of man in a white robe with golden sashes, with eyes of fire and hair of wool. He also mentioned the seven stars that were in the being's right hand. This totally startled me. John was describing the heavenly being I encountered in my dream. I like to think Jesus Christ himself came and anointed me with His peace. After all, I did call on the name Jesus while I was in my midnight hour.

I am so grateful to have had this experience. To think that Jesus actually heard me and cared deeply enough for me to come and personally give me peace, makes me grateful. Had He not come, I might have been the one to end up in a mental institution. Who knows? Now I truly know what Jesus meant when He said, *"My peace I leave with you, my peace I give to you. I do not give to you as the world gives"* (John 14:27). From that day on I was set free, and I felt so much better.

If you are one who is facing great tribulations in your life, I urge you to ask Jesus to anoint you with the gift of peace. He will do it. If He did it for me, He will do it for you. Peace is freely given to us because it is a necessary tool for our survival. So many of us have not experienced the true gift of peace that comes from Jesus Christ but now is the time to affirm the peace that Jesus desires to give you. All you have to do is just ask quietly in your heart or before you lay down to sleep. Once you ask, begin to affirm the peace of God into your life.

Speak these words of peace into your life.

Today, I welcome the peace that comes from the hand of God. Today I will think thoughts of peace. I will speak thoughts of peace; for today, I will be at peace. My mind is at peace. There is peace in me. There is peace in my home. There is peace at my workplace. There is peace all around me. Today, I welcome the gift of peace, which surpasses all understanding. Today, I have peace just knowing. Today, I have peace just being still. Today, I have peace because God is God. Peace be still. Peace be still. Peace be still! And so it is.

9. Guidance from the Holy Spirit

However, when He, the spirit of truth has come, He will guide you into all truth; for He will not speak on His own authority, but whatever He hears, He will speak and tell you things to come (John 16:13).

The Holy Spirit has many responsibilities. One of His responsibilities is to lead and guide people into the truth about themselves and the truth about the love of God. He is known for being the spirit of truth because He knows all things that are to take place in your life and has been given the task to make them known to you when it concerns your future. Why do you think He desires to show you things to come? Fortunately, it is not the will of God for anyone to perish, suffer everlasting damnation, waste away, live a life without meaning or purpose, or self-destruct. If God does not desire that any of His children perish, you can rest assured He will keep His word by sending the Holy Spirit to constantly lead and guide us in the way we should go to prevent us from turning away from the truth. God assigned the Holy Spirit the task to remind you of the word of God. For example, if you ask God to help you understand things and situations that make absolutely no sense to you, the Holy Spirit will remind you to trust in the Lord with all your heart. He does this to help us remain steadfast in God and to keep us from doing the things that we should not do. That is why it is crucial we always make time to study God's word (planting seeds of knowledge).

Studying God's word and writing it upon the tablet of your heart will help you when you need it most. If you do not know God's word, how can the Holy spirit remind you of it when you are in distress? You and the Holy Spirit must work together. If you do your part, He will do His.

So many times the Holy Spirit has tried to help us, but how many of those times have we actually listened to His guidance? In my experience, there have been many occasions the Holy Spirit has helped me. There have been times when He has warned me of danger, and there have been times He has shown me many good things. Whenever we have instructions from the Holy Spirit, no matter what the situation is, we must be obedient to His leading. We have to trust that He is directing our lives. We must not grieve the Holy Spirit by being disobedient. When we are disobedient to His directions, we end up saying and doing things we regret later. If the Spirit says be quiet, then close your mouth. If the Spirit says speak, then speak. If the Spirit says move, then move. When you learn to follow His leading, you are only moving towards your purpose and your destiny.

You may be wondering how to know if you are really hearing from the Holy Spirit. My best answer is this: first receive Him, and from there on, practice makes perfect. Years ago, I began to believe the Holy Spirit was actually showing me things to come. I would have visions while I lay asleep at night, and would awake to have that vision actually play out in the near future, sometimes the next day. So, after several visions that actually happened, I learned that God was communicating with me while I lay asleep at night. God's word proved true. The Holy Spirit was actually showing me things to come. I have had so much experience with my dreams and visions that I can now distinguish a vision from God while I sleep from a normal dream.

God communicates to people in different ways. His best method is when you are asleep. I believe He likes to speak while you sleep because He knows your body is in a resting state. It is quite hard to hear from God while your running around like a chicken with your head cut off. I know we all have busy lives, but we must make time to hear guidance from God. We are more likely to hear sound instruction from Him when our minds and spirits are in a resting state. When the flesh is relaxed, the Spirit then awakens and is open for clear communication. Not everyone will hear from the Lord while they lay asleep at night, so do not feel bad if God does not speak to you then.

God also communicates to people through His word. His word is a very effective way to give you instructions concerning your life. Many people have discovered their purpose in life through a spoken word from the Holy Bible. On several occasions, the Holy Spirit, through written scripture in the bible, has guided me.

Whichever way you may think you are hearing from the Holy Spirit, always make sure what you are hearing lines up with the promises of God for your life written in the bible. If it does not, then it is not the Holy Spirit speaking. Let's use this scripture. *For I know the plans I have for you, plans to give you a future and plans to bring you no harm* (Jeremiah 29:11). This scripture is one of many that helped me to make a conscious effort to remove myself from so much chaos in my life. As I began to study God's word, I happened to come across this particular scripture. As I meditated upon it, I began to examine my present circumstances, and it was so sad to me that not everything I encountered at that time lined up with God's word. I remember thinking, *Oh my God, God has a plan for me, and all this dysfunctional bizarre stuff I am involved in is not part of that plan.*

How did I know this? All the chaos I was involved in was not leading me towards a future of prosperity, hope, and happiness. My behaviors did not line up with God's word. In fact, I was heading towards a self-destructive future. I know now that the Holy Spirit was not leading me then the devil led me. When I realized this, I began to make changes through a lot prayer and total reliance on the Holy Spirit for guidance and help. To this day, when I feel myself on the verge of giving up, the Holy Spirit brings this wonderful life-changing scripture to my remembrance. Then a brand new hope fills my heart.

I encourage you to rely on the guidance that comes from the Holy

Spirit. Take advantage of this special guidance. Learn to trust Him, and learn to ask Him for advice and help. When people come into your life, ask the Holy Spirit to reveal to you the kind of spirit that resides within them. I promise you, He will. It will be up to you to listen. I have learned from many hard learned lessons to listen to the voice of the Holy Spirit. He will never fail you. I have learned to trust and believe what He shows me about my future, others, and me. A sister in Christ used to tell me, "My spirit never tricks me."

I love those words she said because they are words of truth. In other words, she was saying, "The Spirit never lies."

Because the Holy Spirit fills us, and He remains with us and in us, He will never lie or deceive us.

You may be wondering whether you are filled with the Holy Spirit or not. If you are not sure, all you have to do is ask God to fill you with the comforter that Jesus promised to all who believed. You do not have to go running all around the church, but you can if you want. You do not have to do anything special. Just ask God to fill you with the Holy Spirit and He will. Repeat these words: *Father in the name of Jesus Christ I receive by faith the Mighty Counselor, known as the Holy Ghost who is my comforter. I invite you Holy Spirit to dwell within me and show me all that you have received from my Father to make known to me. My heart will be receptive when you speak, and I will obey the words you speak so that I may prosper and do well in the land that I dwell in now. In Jesus'name, I receive the Holy Spirit.*

Speak these words into your life today.

The wisdom of God now leads me through the great and mighty counsel of the Holy Spirit. A higher level of intelligence guides my thoughts. The truth is audible to my ears. My words are being guided to speak in truth, love, and wisdom. My steps are being ordered and divinely led by the power of the Holy Spirit. My day is being guided by fate and purpose. The Holy Spirit is now reminding me that there is a purpose and a great plan for my life. Thank you Holy Spirit for leading me to that great place of peace, happiness, success, prosperity, and joy! Lead me Great Spirit, for in you I do trust. Lead me Great Spirit. Show me all things to come. Lead me Great Spirit, for my life is not my own. Lead me Great Spirit toward my purpose and my call. Lead me Great Spirit into greatness. In Jesus' name it is done.

10. Affirmation of Freedom

Stand fast therefore in the liberty by which Christ has made us free, and do not be entangled again with a yoke of bondage. Therefore whom the Son makes free, he is free indeed (Galatians 5:1).

Freedom is a condition of one's mind and one's spirit. Freedom is the ability to communicate your thoughts and desires to others without feeling guilty and ashamed for doing so. Freedom is also the ability to be who you desire to be without any cares of what others may think of you. Freedom allows you to be yourself without any remorse.

Do you know how many people long to be free? So many of us live a life chained in bondage. It is very sad to say, but most of these bound people are followers of Jesus Christ. Why is this so? Did Jesus not die to set us free from being slaves to sin? Did Jesus not die so that we may have life and have it more abundantly? Doesn't God's word say that where the Spirit of the Lord is there is liberty? If all of these scriptures claim that we are to be free, then why are so many followers of Jesus in bondage? The truth is that so many believers claim that Jesus is in their lives, but they have not received nor have they understood the true purpose for Him dying on the cross just to be a part of their lives. I do not think it is fair to blame Christians for this lack of knowledge concerning their freedom, however, I believe religion is to be blamed.

Religion teaches us that we cannot do this and that. Religion teaches us that we cannot express ourselves because it is considered un-Christ like. Religion also convinces people that they have to represent Christ in a certain way. By doing this, they somehow become lost in their religious beliefs, and they spiritually become bonded with shackles and chains because they cannot be free to be who they really are in Christ, because they are slaves to the fear inside of themselves of what others may think of their decision to live a life of freedom. God wants us to enjoy our lives freely. So many people are living in bondage due to their religious beliefs.

I must say that if I gave my life as a sacrificial ransom so that other lives would be saved from damnation and people could enjoy a life of abundance and feel free in their souls, I would expect them to be doing just that. Jesus spoke the truth to His followers in love because He was free to do so. Jesus did not bite his tongue. He spoke His mind. As I study the ministry of Jesus, I realize that He had to have a free spirit, because there were times when He would cry out the truth to God's people. Can you imagine Jesus actually crying out in a loud voice the truth about God? It must have been an awesome thing. I know this was freedom. Jesus was not concerned with what people thought of Him; He was concerned with their souls.

Have you been able to share a bit of truth with someone lately? Were you aware that just one word of truth spoken from your lips in honesty and love could change someone's life? Were you aware that God wants to use you as a vessel to help change peoples lives? God's wants to use you to heal others. If we desire to minister effectively, we must first learn to live and walk in a life of freedom. People who are in bondage are slaves to fear. They are too afraid to experience the repercussions of expressing the words they speak. It is kind of like being in love so deeply, but never having a chance to tell the one you love, "I love you."

And when you finally get the courage to do so, it is too late. What is the harm in telling another person you love them? Is not love a commandment from God?

Freedom gives you the ability to be who you are, do what it is you like to do, and accomplish things without worrying what others think of you. Now I am not saying that as a Christian, you should not live a self-disciplined life, because you should, but I am saying that you should not be so disciplined that you cannot enjoy the freedom that is affiliated with Christ. The bible says: *Whom the Son sets free, is free indeed* (John 8:36). Life was not designed to be all about hurt and pain. Life was designed for you to have good times as well. If you feel like laughing, you should be free to do so. If you feel like being silly, you also have the freedom to do so. If you feel like you need to praise God really loud and get out of control, you should be able to do so without giving one thought about what someone is going to think of you. You do have the freedom to make time to enjoy yourself while you are alive.

Here are the steps to walking in freedom. The first thing you need to do in order to be free is to receive the freedom that comes from the blood of Christ shed on the cross for you. Write these words on the tablet of your heart: Jesus came so that you may have life (growth, the evidence of being alive), and have it more abundantly (a surplus, an overflow of,). Jesus died to set you free. As we prepare to meet Him one day, we are to prepare in total freedom. He died to set our souls free. He died so that we would not be condemned to everlasting darkness. He died so that you might have a chance to express the divine power of God in you freely and that is love, peace, joy, self-control, patience, and all of the other fruits of the spirit. He died so that you would be able to do greater works than He did, freely. When you receive the gift of freedom, you are then released from people bondage.

You must come to terms with who you are. You must get to know yourself. Who are you? What is your purpose for being alive? What makes you happy? What makes you sad? You must figure out the essence of who you are. One who is to be free, must first learn who he is. The next step towards freedom is to learn to communicate thoroughly. You must learn to speak from the depths of your soul with love and respect towards others. When people make you feel a certain way, it is your responsibility to learn to communicate exactly how they are making you feel. If they are making you feel wonderful, then express that. If they are making you feel ill, then express that.

Always express yourself in a way that you would want others to express themselves to you. It would be a good idea to write how you feel on paper, and then in words tell them exactly how you feel. One who learns to communicate effectively is one who is then free from bondage.

Speak these words of freedom into your life today!

Today, I am free. Today, I am at liberty to live my life to the fullest. Today I am at liberty with who I am. Today, I am free to love without the commitment of conditions; I am free to give without selfish expectations, and I am free to receive the harvest of the seeds I have sown. Today, I am free to care less what others think of me about my own choices that God has given me the freedom to make. Thank you great and mighty God for freedom. Today, I am free to explore my spiritual awareness with God in any way I choose without feeling judged or condemned by another. Today, I am free to be all that I can be for God and for me. Today, I am free to share my heart's desires with God and my innermost secrets, for He is trustworthy. Today, I am free to speak a word of truth into someone's life that will be life changing. Today, I am free to believe the greatest things are capable of happening to me and for me. Today, I am free to just be myself. Today, I receive the freedom of Jesus Christ. In Jesus' name, I am now free!

11. Affirmation of Spiritual Awareness

And do this, knowing the time, that now is the time to awake out of sleep; for now our salvation is nearer than we first believed (Romans 13:11).

Spiritual awareness is awakening to your higher self. There is more to you than what you see in the mirror each day. There is a real live spirit man that is wrapped in what you see in the mirror each day. When you begin to tap into your spirit man, all truth about you is revealed. Your greatest potentials can be fulfilled when you awaken to your true self. You then awaken to your divine connection with God. When we become aware of our own greatness, radical changes begin to take place. Once you come in contact with your divine source (God), every good thing that you were equipped with while in the womb must be brought forth to fulfill God's glorious plan.

In order to awaken to your higher self, you must come to the realization that there is a spirit within you who desires the truth. You must accept that your flesh is merely a home for your spirit to reside in while you prepare for eternity. You must begin to feed your spirit and starve your flesh. I do not mean do not eat. I mean you must tune into the desires of your spirit, not your flesh. I understand that we all live in flesh and since we do, we are going to have fleshly desires, but we must desire spirit more than flesh. When we begin to desire the things of the spirit, we become very powerful. In fact, we become so powerful that we are able to tame the desires of our flesh. When we awaken to the spirit, we then have dominion over our flesh. When we concentrate on fulfilling our fleshly desires, our flesh dominates our spirit. The proper way is for our spirit man to dominate our fleshly man. Spirit must rule over flesh. If this is not done then, we are prone for destruction. Your spirit is far more advanced than your flesh, but because you are in a physical body, you are going to be tempted to satisfy the desires of your fleshly appetite more so than your spiritual appetite. This is why God's word encourages to develop an important spiritual fruit, self-control. God urges us to master the sin within ourselves.

Your spirit man knows more than you think. Your spirit knows what purpose it is suppose to be fulfilling here on earth. Each and every day your inner spirit tries to steer you in that direction, but it can only lead you into your assignments if your willing to follow. Because you are in the flesh, you have been given the freedom to make your own choices. The Holy Spirit can become best friends with your spirit man if you allow Him. The Holy Spirit will speak to your spirit not your flesh. This is why it is so important to rise to a level of spiritual awareness that will allow you to hear what the spirit desires to speak.

The Holy Spirit speaks what He hears from the mouth of God and then will speak to your spirit man. Spirit connects with spirit. God is a spirit; therefore, He sends His word forth through His messenger, the Holy Spirit so that He may tell you all the things that He hears from the mouth of God. Do you understand? God's spirit, the Holy Spirit, and your spirit must all connect. When this happens we rise to a higher level of awareness, and we then begin to receive revelations concerning our future.

This is why it is crucial to connect with the spirit of God and allow His spirit to lead you and guide you and not your flesh. Your flesh will really mess up your whole life. Now you now that if you hear someone say they have "heard from God," you understand that it is really the Holy Spirit speaking to their spirit man the message from God. God does not have to speak, but He can if He wants. His voice is very powerful and so deep with vibration, that if we actually heard His voice, it would probably be too much to bear. Do you remember the story of Moses? The people wanted to hear from the Lord themselves. When God began to speak, they could not stand to hear Him. The Lord spoke to His people through Moses. Today, God speaks to His people by the power of the Holy Spirit, His prophets, and His word.

Wouldn't it be amazing if our spirits were on the outside and our flesh was on the inside? We would accomplish so much. Unfortunately, this is not how God designed us. In order to rule the flesh, we must learn to walk in the spirit. In order to rise to a higher level of awareness, we must worship God, in spirit, and in truth. This means you must act as if you are totally a spirit. You must seek for, and chase after the things of the spirit. You must develop a longing within you, which will draw you closer to the divine spirit of God. Begin to seek God (spirit) with all of your heart. Study God's word so that you may discover spiritual things. Begin to talk to God, and talk to the spirit with in you (through prayer) so that you rise to a higher spiritual vibration. Awaken your spirit by seeking your purpose. When you begin to do these things, you will then become aware of just who and what you really are. You will also notice that your flesh has become dominated by your spirit resulting, in miraculous changes. Today awaken the spirit man who lives in side of you. Today, become aware of who you really are!

Affirm spiritual awareness into your life today!

Today, I choose to dominate my flesh by allowing my spirit to rule. Today, I am becoming aware of my spiritual self. Today, I am aware of all the goodness that is waiting to be expelled from within my spirit to love and to help another human being. Today, I am aware of the changes that must take place in my life. Today, I am aware of my own spiritual gifts. Today, I am aware of my own spiritual beauty. Today, I am aware that God my creator is walking along my journey with me each day. Today, I am aware of the presence of my guardian angel. Today, I am keen to all spiritual experiences, which have been designed to help me grow into the person God has intended for me to be. I thank God that I am now awakened to my higher self. In Jesus' name, it is done!

12. Affirmation of Wisdom

Listen, for I speak of excellent things, and from the opening of my lips will come right things. For my mouth will speak truth (Proverbs 8:6).

If we desire to get ahead in life, we must learn to literally love the precious words of wisdom. It is not something for which you have to beg God. God's word assures us that if we ask for wisdom He will freely give it to us and He gives it to us quickly. Reason being, God understands that man is but merely dust, therefore it pleases Him when we humble ourselves and ask him for wisdom and direction in our lives. We should always apply wisdom to our decision-making.

A wise way to make decisions is to line them up with the promises of God. You never want to make a decision that goes against God's word. God wants to direct our steps so that we can receive the promises in His word. When we have certain situations in our lives that we are having difficulty managing, God will freely give us direction. Wisdom will bring us into alignment with God's master plan for our lives. Wisdom will lead us towards financial increase. Wisdom will instruct us on managing our homes, our finances, our marriages, and any area of our lives that He has given us stewardship over. Wisdom also will protect us from dangerous situations that would bring harm to us. Wisdom really should be considered as a friend. Her presence is willing to gently guide anyone who asks for advice. She is the one who assisted God, our creator, in laying the foundations of our earth that we live in today. So why not welcome her sweet presence into your life. Wisdom saves many from death and destruction.

I would like to share a story that my aunt shared with me about a friend of hers. Her friend entered into a building and was getting ready to ride the elevator to another floor. When the elevator doors opened, there was a man standing on the elevator. As she began to enter the elevator, a voice called out to her saying, *"It would not be wise for you to go inside."*

When she heard the voice, she humbled herself and decided to wait on the next one. Another woman got on the elevator and was killed. I believe this was the voice of wisdom speaking to my aunt's friend to save her life. My aunt's friend applied wisdom by obeying the voice that spoke to her spirit. Because she made the wise choice not to enter into the elevator, her life was spared. Any time God speaks to us, we can choose to either be wise and listen or be foolish by being disobedient.

Speak these words of wisdom into your life today!

I now call on the beautiful bountiful presence of wisdom into my life. I welcome wisdom into my home, my finances, my marriage, and all of my affairs. I am now wise because wisdom has made her home with me. I now lay hold of her wonderful words with all my heart. I now keep her commands so that I may live. I will not forsake wisdom, and she and my father are now protecting me. I will love her and because I love wisdom, she and my father shall watch over me. Wisdom is supreme, and now that she resides within me, I too am supreme! Now that I have esteemed her, I am now being exalted. I am now accepting the things she has to say. Now that I have laid a hold of wisdom, I am now blessed. In Jesus' name it is done.

13. Affirmation for the Blessing of Might

The spirit of the Lord shall rest upon him, the spirit of wisdom and understanding, the spirit of counsel and might, the spirit of knowledge and of the fear of the Lord (Isaiah 11:2).

The blessing of might enables you to accomplish the impossible. In the book of Psalms, it is revealed how one might receive the blessing of might. It reads, *Once you spoke in a vision, to your faithful people you said: I have bestowed strength on a warrior, I have exalted a young man from among the people. I have found David my servant and with my sacred oil, I have anointed Him. My hand will sustain Him; surely my arm will strengthen him* (Psalm 89: 19-21).

This strength is known as might. The spirit of might comes directly from the hands of God. Because His strength is all-powerful, when we connect with God, He willingly pours that strength upon us. Might is an extra dose of strength that God gives to his chosen ones to accomplish a great task. God's word says He will strengthen us with his right hand.

To help you better understand this, I have come up with an analogy to make things more clear. From the hands of God comes everything. When we ask God to anoint us with the spirit of might, we ask for an extra dose of strength to accomplish every good work that He has for us to complete. What He does is lay His hands upon us. From His hands comes a special oil that enables us to go forward and fulfill our purpose here on earth. When we receive the blessing of might, it is then when we can stand and say boldly, "I can do all things through Christ who strengthens me."

When God's hand is upon us, we are able to fulfill the awesome plan He has for our lives.

I first learned of the blessing of might from a biblical series that Creflo Dollar taught some time ago. I began to wonder how would I go to college, be a good mother, work to pay bills, make time with God, and make time for me. Although I was doing it, and I knew God was helping me, I did not know that God had placed a special blessing on my life so that the good work He started in me, would be completed. Pastor Dollar taught me that I was to ask for the blessing of might so that I could accomplish everything that God desired me to accomplish. I began to do this and God did give me strength. Receiving knowledge about the blessing of might is one of the best secrets of God that I could have possibly learned. I thank God for this teaching and I encourage you to begin to ask God to pour forth the blessing of might over your life. It is well worth asking. If we desire to accomplish great things, we must have the blessing of might placed upon our lives. If we desire to do all things in Christ, the blessing of might must saturate us.

Speak the blessing of might into your life today!

I now evoke the spirit of might. I am now receiving the special blessing of might. I am now being anointed with the sacred oil of might. In Jesus' name, I will now accomplish the impossible, think the unthinkable, dream the dreams that I dare to dream, be the person God chose me to be, and live the life that God has ordained for me. I now receive the spirit of might. I am now walking on my journey of faith with might. I am conquering all challenges with the spirit of might. I am fighting all the attacks of the enemy with the spirit of might. I am tearing down strongholds with the spirit of might. I am more than a conqueror with the spirit of might. The spirit of might rests upon me. I can do all things through Christ who strengthens me. In Jesus' name, it is done.

14. Affirmation of Will

If you are willing and obedient ye shall eat the good of the land (Isaiah 1: 19).

In order for optimum spiritual growth, a spirit of willingness must reside inside of us. Whatever we decide to do with our lives, we must be willing to make sacrifices to get where we desire to be. You must be willing to make mistakes and learn from them. You must be willing to admit that you have made mistakes. You must be willing to admit when you are wrong. You must be willing to apologize when you say and do things that hurt others. You must be willing to tell the truth. You must be willing to step out and take risks even if what you are doing seems as though it is not making any sense.

Remember that when you are willing God is willing. When you are willing to move out of your past and into you future, God is willing to take the necessary steps and actions to move you into better horizons, but you first must be willing. When you are willing to take risks and step out on faith, God will stretch His hands towards you and bless you because of your faith.

I made God a promise. I promised that if He would somehow work a miracle and move my babies and myself out of the projects, I would go to college and complete my education. I knew I had to go back to school and pursue an education or else my children and I would remain in poverty. I was willing to go back to school, but I knew I could only do it with God's help. How would I pay my bills? Who would stay with my children while I attended school? Could I really handle everything? I had to be willing to surrender all my fears and all my doubts to God, stop asking questions, and just step out in faith.

We must be willing to let go of anything that will interfere with our growth and development. Be willing to let go and surrender all to God. Be willing to surrender your desires to him, your thoughts, and all of your cares to God because He cares for you and is willing to meet you at any point in your life you are at to ensure that your purpose here on earth is fulfilled. Be willing to take risks and chances. You will never know how the outcome of a situation will be if you are not willing to see it all the way through until the end. It all starts with your will to be willing.

Speak these words of willingness into your life.

Today, I am willing to give my best to God. I am willing to do whatever it takes to get where God wants me to be. Today, I am willing to make a change in my life. Today, I am willing to release every thought or imagination that exalts itself against God. Today, I am willing to be still and know that God is God, and that He is in control of my thoughts, words, deeds, and every step I take. Today, I am willing to trust that things are actually working on my behalf and for my good no matter what things look like. Today, I am willing to make the necessary changes that are required for me to succeed in God. Today, I am willing to give. Today, I am willing to receive. Today, I am willing to learn. Today, I am willing to listen to the voice of the Holy Spirit for the guidance of my steps. Today, I am willing to forgive others and myself. Today, I am willing to participate wholeheartedly in my experience of life. Today, I am willing to step out in faith to fulfill my purpose here on earth. In Jesus' name, I am willing.

15. Affirmation of Spiritual Wealth

I know thy works, and tribulations, and poverty, (but thou are rich) (Revelation 2:6).

If you want to become a wealthy person, it is important for you to learn to develop a wealthy spirit. The first thing is to understand that before anything happens in the natural, it must first take place in the spirit. Spiritual wealth has nothing to do with money or how many material things you have. The soul longs to be satisfied with spiritual riches while the flesh desires the riches of this world. Both of these longings are quite natural because we are spiritual beings wrapped up in flesh. It is necessary to find a balance between both of the desires. First and most we should always desire the riches of the spirit rather than the riches of this world. The heavens and the earth shall pass away, but God's word remains forever. The riches of the spirit last forever, but the riches of this world last only for a moment's time.

You gain spiritual wealth only through a spiritual walk with God. Have you ever known people who materially did not seem to have much, but their spirit seemed very wealthy? They seemed to be so happy and so content. It did not seem to bother them that they lacked what you have. Have you ever envied people like this? If you have, you are not alone. People who base their happiness on things that they can see, touch, and feel are usually the people who feel empty on the inside. No material possession can fill the desires of the human spirit. People who strive to fill their spirit with the treasures from heaven are usually the people who are happy and full on the inside.

When we fuel our spirit with the fruits of God's spirit, we become spiritually wealthy.

It is okay to have physical wealth such as money, fancy cars, and a big mansion on the hill. It is not a sin to be rich. However, it is a shame to have all these material things and have a poverty stricken spirit. You are probably wondering what I mean when I say poverty stricken spirit. What I mean is this: To be rich in this world and able to buy anything you want and go any where you desire is great, but it is terrible to be able to do all these things and inside you are bitter, cold, envious, selfish, unloving, sad, arrogant, and hateful. How could a man enjoy his riches, harboring such feelings inside of himself? Yes, he would be rich, but unable to share. Yes, he would be wealthy, but he could not love. What good is it all if you are rich in the physical, yet poor in the spirit?

So many poor people hunger for the riches of this world, and so many rich people would give up all they had just to experience one day of total peace and total love. Who would ever think that there could be balance? It is possible, but few achieve this balance because of their lack of knowledge. First, it is important to understand what makes a person rich in the spirit. The first thing is the Love of God. There is no greater wealth than God's love. I do not care how much money a man may have, if he does not have the love of God in his heart, he is poor. From the love of God comes the fruit of the spirit.

Joy is also an attribute of spiritual wealth. In Joy, there is strength, and in strength, there is power.

The peace of God is what sustains a man when great trials and tribulations fall upon him. If a rich man has many riches, yet he has no peace, if he should lose all he has, his mind would also be lost. Which is more important? A troubled lost mind or a mind that is kept in perfect peace. A wealthy spirit is prone to long-suffering. Long-suffering teaches you patience, perseverance, and self control. Long-suffering enables us to endure all losses, hardships, and various trials. Long-suffering will enable us to keep on pressing towards our calling in Christ Jesus. A wealthy spirit works toward kindness. There is no room for cruelty. A wealthy spirit brings forth goodness from within itself. It seeks to do good on all occasions and is faithful to what is right and true continuously.

God desires us to be wealthy. He desires us to have nice homes and nice cars. However, He is not pleased when we desire physical riches more than we desire spiritual riches. A wealthy spirit is far more valuable than the riches of this world. The riches of this world will soon pass away and you and I will have to depart from them. A wealthy spirit can be achieved and mastered here on earth and taken on to eternal life with Jesus Christ. The riches of the spirit are the only riches that are ours to keep. We will never have to depart from them. For they shall go with us into eternity.

Speak these words of spiritual wealth into your life:

I am already rich. I am rich in my mind, my body, and my spirit. I am now being filled with the love of God, for the love of God makes me rich. I am now being filled with the joy of the Lord, for the joy of the Lord is my strength. I am now being filled with the peace of God, for the peace of God makes me rich. I am now bringing forth the fruits of the spirit, for the fruits of God's spirit make me rich. In Jesus' name, I am spiritually wealthy.

16. Affirmation of Faith

But without faith it is impossible to please him (Hebrews 11:6).

The woman came and knelt before Him."Lord help me!" she said.

He replied, "It is not right to take the children's bread and toss it to their dogs."

"Yes, Lord," she said, "but even the dogs eat the crumbs that fall from their master's table."

Then Jesus answered, "Woman, you have great faith! Your request is granted."

Her daughter was healed that very hour.

Faith is what touches the heart of God. For we know that if we are to ask anything of God, we must believe that He is God and He will reward those who diligently seek him. Without faith, it is impossible to please the Lord. God's righteous one will live by faith. It should not be hard to comprehend the reasons that God requires us to have faith when approaching Him. We cannot see God, but we know He is there. How do we know? We can feel His presence with us. No one has ever seen the wind, but we feel its powerful gestures almost all the time. It takes faith to know God. When we begin to believe that He really does exist, something very magical happens. God begins to slowly reveal himself to us little by little. He begins to show physical proof that He is real and He is God, but these magical experiences can only be revealed to those who believe. I believe that when we constantly seek God, He is pleased. He then begins to bring to pass all of His promises to the ones who love Him. Faith is not a form of magic, but when a person begins to see the results of his faith being manifested, it seems as if it is magic.

Many people believe if they have faith in the things they desire then all of their desires will happen. There is nothing wrong with believing this, but if the things we desire do not happen, where does that leave a person? Sometimes they get mad at God and say, "Forget this faith stuff, because it does not work anyway."

It is inappropriate to believe that something you desire to happen in your life will happen without believing in the one force that is able to make it happen. Many people say they have faith, but in what do they have faith? It, him, her, and that it is going to happen is what most people have faith in. I do not believe we do this intentionally, but it is imperative for us to learn how to operate in faith the correct way if we desire to see our desires manifested.

The first step to operate in faith is to have faith in God. You may be thinking, I do have faith in God. I will say it again. Have faith in God! You see, having faith in God and having faith that something will happen are two very different things. Understand the omnipotent power of God. He is creator of the heavens, the earth, the moon, the sun, the stars, the waters, the wind, the trees, people, and everything that your mind can ever dream. He is actually the air that you breathe. He rules out all things to come in your life. He decides the day you are to be born, and He decides the hour your spirit is to depart from this earth and return to Him. He examines your heart every morning before you even think about waking. It is His decision if you are to awake to another day.

In this, you are to place your faith. Faith is the substance of things hoped for; it is the evidence of the things not seen. The substance that underlies all that we will ever hope for is God. The evidence of these things you do not see that come into manifestation is the work of God. This is why the word of God always tells us to put our hope in God. It clearly tells us to have faith in God. It says trust in God. When you invest all your hopes and dreams in God, they have no choice but to manifest themselves as the desires of your heart.

Say for instance, a woman is in a marriage that is on the way to divorce court. She desires her marriage to be saved. She is using all the faith that she has to believe that the marriage will not end in divorce. Her husband is acting up, and he wants the divorce. He does not desire to be with her anymore. Can her faith in her husband changing save the marriage? No. What can save the marriage is her faith in God. She must believe that God, and God only, is in control of the situation. She must understand that only the power of God can give her husband a change of heart. She must surrender the desire to try to save the marriage herself. She must be quiet and allow God's purpose to happen. She must continue to pray faithfully without ceasing. She must understand that if she is doing what is required of her then God will do His part.

If the marriage does end in divorce, she must not blame it on her faith. She must not get angry with God. She must come to understand that God allowed the divorce for a specific reason. She must be spiritually mature enough to begin to search for her new purpose as a single divorced woman. She must have faith that God is God and He knows what is best for her. She must always have faith that God is God and whatever He allows her to experience, is in His divine will. A woman, who places her faith in God and believes that He really is in control, will be stronger and fortified in her spirit to be able to go on with her life and live productively after divorce.

Another thing to remember is that faith will not get you things that are not meant to be yours. God has ordained things for each of us. It is our responsibility to commune with God to figure out which paths to take in life. Through prayer, God will reveal our purpose to us, allowing us a chance to make His plans for us come into fruition.

Another thing to remember is to have fun with your faith. Go ahead and be radical because you never know what is in store for you. It is important to have fun in God because if you do not then you become bored. I remember a girlfriend and I became so stirred up in our faith we actually drove down to the car lots where our dream cars were. We took our bibles and spoke the word of God concerning faith as we walked around the cars in circles. We were yelling and screaming things like, "We have what we say, and we say these cars are ours in Jesus' holy name!"

This was actually the best time I had in a long time. Dr. Creflo Dollar was teaching a biblical series on faith and we just ran wild with it. We were laughing so hard, because we just knew that we looked like raving religious nuts, but we did not care because our hearts were filled with radical faith.

Karen needed a car. She had been without a car for sometime and she was praying to God for her dream car. I already had a car, but I was praying to God for my dream car. About a month or so later, I remember telling her to go and get her dream car. She went to the same car lot that we went to a month prior and she came home with her brand new dream car! We both praised God and were so happy over the whole experience. This really increased our faith.

Karen and I also believed that we would one day live in a mansion on a hill, so of course one day we drove into a rich neighborhood, stood in front of this beautiful huge mansion, and we praised God that one day we too would be living in one of those mansions. My children were praising God for our new mansion as well. I can remember a man looking out of his window and the good Lord only knows what he was thinking. We were having so much fun being radical. We were hoping he did not have us arrested. We laughed and laughed until our stomachs ached. The whole experience of these stretches of our faith was heartfelt, exciting, and fun. Who would ever think a poor single mother of two would actually be living in a mansion of well over a million dollars? I actually believed that if it is God's will then it would one day be so. I believed that somehow God was going to see me out there at that mansion stretching my faith, and that one day He was going to move my children and me into a mansion. I did not expect man to do it, but I expected and believed that God could and would do it if it was His will. This is radical, but when you love God with all your heart and soul and you believe that He has the power and the ability to make anything happen, then you too cannot help but to become a radical woman or man of God. It is okay to stretch your faith because reaching for the impossible actually will bless your soul and will touch God's funny bone. I believe we actually had God laughing that day because we sure could not stop.

Remember to place your faith totally in God, and if what you are praying to God for aligns itself with God's covenant plan for your life, you can count on it to happen. Have faith in God. Have fun in God. Have peace in God. Have joy knowing that with God all things are truly possible, and since all things are possible, anything that you can imagine can be so, but try your very best to understand the will of God for your life. It is okay to dream big dreams and think big things because God wants to give you good things, and a good life. Just make sure the things you desire line up with His word. Be sure that what you're asking for will bless others as it will bless you. Be sure that what you want is not for selfish gain. Because when the time comes for God to examine your heart, you will want Him to find your intentions blameless in His eyes. So have faith, live faith, walk in faith, speak in faith, and believe that God is touched by your acts of faith.

Speak these words of faith into your life today!

Today, I receive the gift of faith. I have faith in God not man. I have faith that I will receive whatever God has ordained me to receive. Today, I choose to live a faith filled life. With God, nothing shall be impossible. I shall receive the full fledge promises of God. I exist by faith, I am breathing by faith, and I am moving into my appointed destiny by faith. I am faith. I am all that God says I am because of faith. I speak this and by the power of my words, it is so! Faith, faith, faith, I speak faith, faith, faith, I live by faith, faith, faith, faith, I am faith, faith, faith, faith. In Jesus' name, I am a woman (man) of faith!

17. Affirmation of Self-Forgiveness

Self forgiveness paves the way for new beginnings.

It all begins with self. I know you have heard someone say, "I had to learn to love myself," or "I had to learn to be myself," or "I had to put me first."

Another important thing we must learn to do, is forgive ourselves. I always hear people say things like, "I had to work really hard to forgive that person." This may be true, but I hardly ever hear people say, " I had to forgive myself."

'It does all begin with self. It all begins with you. There are many things that you may have said or done in your past that you cannot seem to forgive yourself for. We all have pasts. We all have done things that make us feel ashamed and unworthy. In order to heal from our pasts, we must learn to face them and forgive ourselves, because if we do not, we will not be able to move into the future God has planned for us.

Satan finds great joy in throwing our pasts in our face. He does this to prevent us from moving towards the future. It's the devil's job to accuse you so you can live each day of your life feeling unworthy and guilty about your past. He is quite clever, and he knows all about the spirit world and all about God. After all, he was one of God's most precious angels. He knows that if you hold ill feelings towards yourself, then there is no promising future for you.

When you walk around every day holding your past against you, and when you allow your past to stop you from moving forward in life, you have become a pillar of salt spiritually. You may not be aware of this, and I pray that what I am about to say will be a spiritual revelation for you. There is a great possibility that you have not forgiven yourself for the things you have done in the past. I do not care how horrible the thing you have done may be, I do not care how shameful it is. If God forgave you through the blood of Jesus Christ, then you can forgive yourself. If you have faith that your sins have been forgiven through the name of Jesus Christ, then why are you being so hard on yourself?

A young man I met shortly after I arrived to Atlanta, who became one of my most valued friends, died in a car accident in 1998. His death devastated me. Jay, my friend, came over to my apartment to visit me. After a four-year friendship, Jay and I decided that we wanted to be together. Jay had always been there for me no matter what. I believe I had the dysfunctional bad boy - good girl syndrome. Even though I knew Jay was the man I should have settled down with, I just could not. I was only eighteen when we met. I had just moved to Atlanta and I wanted to party. I did not want to settle down right away. Through it all Jay had always checked up on me. He always told me that when I was ready, we could be together and he would give me anything my heart desired. My self-esteem was so low back then I could not accept anything good. When he told me I was beautiful, I did not believe him. When he said he would do anything for me, I would not let him. When he finally explained to me that he was in love with me, I did not believe him.

I remember the night he told me he loved me. I said, "Jay, how can you love me? We never have made love to each other."

He said he did not need to make love to me to be in love with me. I had no clue what he was talking about. I had always linked sex to love. My mind was convinced that sex meant love, and you can only be in love with someone if you have sex with them. He told me he loved my personality and the spirit within me. He looked past all of my dysfunctional behaviors and loved me in spite of them. He saw the goodness and potential in me and fell in love with my soul. Unfortunately, I was unable to recognize that this man loved me. I was too dysfunctional at that time. Not only did he say he loved me, he showed me that he loved me. Throughout every event in my life, I remember him being there either with me or for me.

When I finally decided that I should give him a chance, he was living with another woman. Years had gone by, and I really could not blame him for moving on with his life. He was truthful with me and told me that the woman who he was living with was a marriage arranged by his parents. He told me he was not in love with her and he refused to marry her. He explained the difficulty of the situation because her parents and his parents were close, and they put them together. I wanted things to work out with us, but I was not willing to stand for him living with another woman. So we called it quits until he could get things straight. After some time, I became involved with someone else and became pregnant with Nia. When I told him he was disappointed, but he looked me in my eyes and said, "Well, I guess I will have two babies to take care of." It was at that moment I knew that I was going to have to learn to accept him. It was then when I realized he was the man I should have been with all along. It was then when I decided that I wanted to spend the rest of my life with him.

He told me that he arranged to move out of his living conditions very soon. I told him that was fine. One evening, I was not in a very good mood. I guess I felt as though he would never leave that woman or it was not happening fast enough for me. I was under a lot of pressure and I wanted him to hurry up and move out from the other woman's house. He came to my apartment one evening, and I asked him would he be mad if I asked him to leave and not come back until he straightened things out with her. I thought if I threw him out, things would move along more quickly. I remember him asking me, "Is that what you want?"

I said, "Yes."

He quietly left, and as I turned the lock, I somehow knew it was the last time I would ever see him. I opened the door and watched him leave, and I wanted to say something, but I could not.

Usually, we would make up shortly after we would have arguments but a couple of months passed by and I began to worry. My pride would not allow me to call him. I felt if he really loved me, he should be the one to call me. So a few more months passed by, and I decided that I would have to call him.

I was about six months pregnant with Nia. It was a Saturday morning when I decided I wanted my friend back. I was going to call him and ask him to forgive me for the way I behaved. Therefore, I called his dad because when I paged him, the number was out of service. I called his parents' house and some woman answered the phone. When I asked to speak to Jay, she said with a nasty voice, "Jay is dead."

In shock, I said, "Let me speak to his father."

His father got on the phone and told me the most dreadful news I ever heard. He said, "I am sorry, Melissa, but Jay died in a car accident some months ago."

I was very shocked. His dad said they had no way of contacting me. I could not believe that he was gone. I did not even get the chance to say goodbye. The last time we saw each other I threw him out of my house. What was I to do? I cried for several months, which put strain on my pregnancy. I was so sad. I drove all the way out of state to his gravesite and lay over it sobbing endless tears for hours telling him how sorry I was for being so ugly. I knew all the tears in the world could not bring my friend back. He was gone; just like that. The only man that claimed to love me was dead. I blamed myself. It was entirely my fault. I found out that he died a few days after he left my house. I had caused him so much grief that he wrecked.

I held myself responsible for his death. This is what I had convinced myself. I did not understand back then that his time was up. It was his time to go. I hated myself for the way I behaved. I believed God was punishing me for everything I had done wrong in the past. I decided I would never forgive myself for treating my friend the way I did. I did not think God would forgive me either. I just knew this was the most unforgivable thing I could ever do. I thought it was my fault he died. I remember thinking I should have been more patient with him; after all, he was always so patient with me. Every single day I held myself accountable for his death. I was so miserable.

One night as I lay asleep, I dreamed I was talking with someone. At that moment, I was unaware of who it was. My spirit was carried away to another place and this person and I were together.

I was asking the person different questions about heaven. I asked, "Do you like it better here than when you were on earth?"

He said, "Let's just say I know more now than I knew when I was on earth."

I asked him what kinds of things did he know. He said, "Oh, things like reincarnation."

I asked him did God and Jesus really exist. He said, "Yes. God sits on the throne, and Jesus is in control of the afterlife and thereon."

Now the next question I asked him is sort of out of line but I have to be honest because I did ask him. I asked him "Do we get to have sex here?"

He quickly said, "No! None of that here!"

I do not know what made me ask such a question. I did not realize I was talking to Jay until I asked Him if he ever received the flowers and card I lay at his gravesite. I do not know what happened, but it's like we both concentrated with our minds on the place we wanted to be and we were there. When we opened our eyes, we were above his gravesite. We zoomed in on the headstone, he picked up my card, read it, then smiled at me and said thank you. After that, I woke up, and I was so happy. I knew my friend was in heaven with Jesus. I knew he was okay. I also knew that he was not angry with me for kicking him out of my house. I was then able to release all the guilt, and finally forgive myself.

This experience helped me to heal from all the hurt and pain that I felt all those months not knowing if my friend was okay. It was as if God gave me a chance to say goodbye to my friend. I believe God allowed him to visit me because He knew that it was detrimental to my well-being. God is so faithful and compassionate. If I not had that one last moment in my dreams with my friend, I would not have been able to forgive myself and move on with my life.

You may not have an experience as this one, but you do not have to in order to forgive yourself. You need only to understand that God promises us in His word that He will blot out our sins and remember them no more. Because of Jesus, you can ask the Father for forgiveness in His son's name. If God can forgive you, no matter how serious your offenses are then you can forgive yourself. I was unaware at the time my friend passed, all I had to do was ask God for forgiveness and then forgive myself. I walked around several months in severe depression, sadness, and guilt. This experience taught me to always end things in love. This tragedy taught me to try my best to have an attitude of humility. I learned to never let my pride get in the way of saying, "I apologize."

Unfortunately, because I could not humble myself, I never got a chance to tell my best friend I was sorry for my ugly behavior that last evening that we were to ever see each other again. Trust me, there is no greater pain than to have someone you love leave this earth and your last words were not word spoken in love.

Fortunately, you do not have to take the same path I took. However, you can begin today to cleanse your spirit. I have heard many people say that we are our worst enemy. It is true. Many times, we are unhappy and miserable because subconsciously, we are holding ill feelings not only towards others but also towards ourselves. I challenge you to begin to examine the depths of your soul to figure out if you have been very hard on yourself because of your past failures and mistakes. Beating up on yourself and holding negative feelings towards yourself defeats the purpose of the crucifixion of our Lord and savior Jesus the Christ. Jesus died so that you may be forgiven for your iniquities and that you may be set free. You are not free if you are holding yourself in chains because of the things you have done in the past. Begin to look at yourself in the mirror and ask God to forgive you and then you forgive you. Speak affirmations of forgiveness to yourself. Cry if you must, and cry hard if you have to, but forgive yourself for your past mistakes, and learn the lesson taught in each of them because God is ready to take you to higher dimensions in your spiritual walk with Him.

Speak these words of self-forgiveness into your life today.

Today, I will no longer hold thoughts and feelings of unforgiveness toward myself. I forgive myself for the things I have done to hurt others and myself as well. I forgive myself for all the times I have abused others physically, mentally, and spiritually. I forgive myself for allowing others to abuse me physically, mentally, and spiritually. I forgive myself for speaking negatively about others as well as my own self. I forgive myself for any dishonoring act that I have done to anyone including myself. I forgive myself! I forgive myself! I forgive myself! Just as God forgave me, now I am forgiven, and so it has been established. Now I am free. In Jesus' name it is done!

18. Affirmation of Forgiveness of Others

For if you forgive men their trespasses, your heavenly Father will also forgive you. But if you forgive not men their trespasses, neither will your Father forgive your trespasses (Matthew 6:14-15).

"I do not understand why I have to forgive her. She abandoned me. I hate her. How could she walk out on her own children?"

I used to make excuses, using those resentful words, for not being able to forgive my mother for leaving me when I was only five years old. I held her accountable for my uncle's sexually violating me. I held her responsible for my self-destructive behaviors such as alcoholism and promiscuity. I actually became ill every time I saw her. Being around her stirred up so much anger in my spirit. All I knew is that because of her negligence I suffered tremendously. As far as my memory allows me to recall, I was dropped off at my mother's brother and his wife's home one evening. I stayed there a while. They had kids of their own. I have a very vague memory of my time with them, but I do remember it was pleasant and to this day when I think about them, I feel a sense of peace.

The horror started when I went to live with my grandparents and my father when I was five years old. I missed my mom. I was more familiar with her than my two younger siblings. They went to live with my aunt, which was one of the most terrible choices any parent could ever decide to make.

My grandfather was more like a father to me. He spent a great deal of time with me. We had a lot of fun together. At that time, he was a pastor of a small church in Marin City, and it is because of him I found God. We used to travel to church across the Golden Gate Bridge on the bus. I enjoyed this. I remember the bridge would actually swing back and forth, as I looked down at the salty gray oceans of the bay. I looked forward to each Sunday because we would always go to Carl Jr.'s to have breakfast. My grandfather took me to many places during the summers. I can remember him preplanning for us all throughout the year. We spent our summers traveling to places such as the zoo, the fair, Marine World, and many other fun places. My grandfather assumed the role as my father because even though my dad lived in the same house with me, he was severely devastated that my mom left him with three small children. He spent a lot of time away from me. I only saw him for a few minutes each day then he would go off to places I knew nothing about. I sometimes heard him discussing something called the NCO Club.

One of my uncles began touching me in my groin area in the basement of my grandfather's house shortly after I arrived. He would sit me on his lap and rub me between my thighs. Each time it happened I remember him getting closer and closer to my vaginal areas. I was only five at the time, and I remember him always saying, "Do not tell anyone. This is our game we play," or something of that nature.

I am not sure how long this went on, but I know he was caught fondling me one night by my two aunts. I guess they noticed I had been missing in action. All I can remember is when they caught him. He never did those things to me again. I do not know why they did not tell my grandfather or my dad. I guess it was just too embarrassing for the whole family and since my grandfather was a pastor, it probably would have been even more embarrassing. I was really too young at the time to have a say so in the matter, however, I still remember the things he did to me very clearly.

Another molestation incident I recall is one that actually frightened me terribly. My grandmother allowed me to spend the night with my godmother. We had a lot of fun that evening. As I lay asleep, I felt something rubbing and kissing all over my legs and feet. I awoke in horror; one of my uncles was actually caressing and kissing my legs and my feet. I screamed and he stopped. I was so scared. It was my other uncle. God only knows how long he was caressing me before I awoke. I believe he was a friend of my godmother's husband because I do recall him spending time over her house as well.

I was about eight years old and was able to confront him for his actions. Fearfully and puzzled, I asked him why did he do those things to me, and he said I was making it up. However, deep in my heart I knew I was not. I never told anyone because it seemed as if nothing would happen. I do not know why I did not tell my grandfather or my dad about this incident. I guess I was afraid and felt helpless.

At the age of nine, I was sent to live with my aunt. This is where my sister and brother lived. The whole time I lived there was a living nightmare. My sister was a baby and stayed right under my aunt, who was deeply involved in the church and spent a lot of time there. While she was away, the beatings took place. My cousin used to make us fight each other. She also used to make us put our faces in hot water. Her brother raped my brother, and I couldn't do anything to help him. I remember one Saturday my cousin and I were home alone. He came upstairs to my room and told me to take off my clothes. I refused. I remember him saying, "Come on, Melissa, it's your turn. You know what you got to do." As I watched him prepare himself, he said, "Melissa, if you do not pull down your panties and let me do it to you, you will not get any ice cream," (or something of that nature), and at the age of nine, I was fed up with having to fight for my pureness, my virginity, and my innocence.

I remember thinking, as I saw that he was ready to penetrate me, *No more! I will not allow this to happen to me ever again!* I looked at my cousin and told him that I did not care if he gave me ice cream or not. I was not letting him have sex with me. I told him that if he did not leave me alone I was going to tell his mom. I quickly ran out the bedroom door, down the stairs, and outside to play. I did not come back home until I knew for sure my aunt would be home and I was safe at least for the evening. I spent a lot of time outside when my aunt was away. I feared sexual abuse while she was away. I could not tell her because she would threaten me and cover her son's tracks as she always did.

From that time on, I did not let anyone else in my family put their hands on me. I never allowed myself to be alone with any of my uncles and cousins. I used to lie in my bed at night and cry endless tears. I wondered if God would come and rescue me from all the hurt and pain. I always told myself that as soon as I became an adult, I was going to move far away from my family.

I tried to live a normal life as a child, but it was very difficult. My aunts would always tell me how fat I was. When it was time to go shopping for school clothes, they would get together in my grandmother's living room and say that they were going to take me to the pudgy girls' clothing store. They would laugh right in my face and say what a shame it was that I was so round and fat. I would sit there, hold my head down, and feel so bad. Little did they know all of the emotional abuse made me very mean. I hated all of them.

One of my aunts used to perm my hair. I had a lot of hair, and at the age of ten, I did not know how to comb it. It was time for my aunt to relax it again, and when she went through my hair, she found tangles and knots. She became enraged and started beating me all over my head with her fists. She beat me on my back and slapped my face while screaming, "You better learn how to comb this mess, you lazy heifer."

While she was beating me, I could not cry. I just held it all in and waited until she was finished. I thought to myself, "It will all be over one day. One day, I will never have to see these people again."

All of my aunts got together, talked about the shape of my body, and laughed at me. They told me that my head was too big and my face was shaped funny. No one ever told me anything good about myself. All I knew was that I was a greedy, fat, weird-shaped, funny-faced, knotty-headed girl. Now that I am an adult, I put it all together from living and learning. My aunts were all dark-skinned and had nappy hair. Here I was, this half-breed child with a beautiful complexion, big brown eyes, and beautiful curly hair, and they despised me. They made me think the worst of myself to destroy my self-esteem and it worked.

The emotional and mental damage was done. I was actually fighting for my innocence. I was struggling to keep my mental sanity as a little girl. I thought families were suppose to love each other not try to sex each other up and tear each other down emotionally. I was deeply hurt. Anger towards my father settled in because when he finally found out about the sexual abuse, he did not do anything to protect me or stand up for me. I remember him actually watching football games with my uncles as if he was saying, "Go ahead do whatever you wish to my daughter. She is of no value to me."

I began to secretly hate him for not protecting me. I hated my aunts for messing up my mind. As you can see, I had some forgiving to do. I hated my mother, my father, my uncles, my cousins, and my aunts, and it all fell back on my mom. If she had only stayed with me! If she had only took me with her! If she just would have been woman enough to deal with the fact that she slept with and married a black man and she had three children that she had to raise, then none of these horrible things would have happened to me.

These are the thoughts I used to think. I needed my mom. Unfortunately, she was nowhere to be found. I grew into an angry and broken adolescent. I was seventeen when I realized that I could not spend the rest of my life hating everyone.

I was planning to move to Atlanta to start a new life for myself. At last, the moment I had waited for, finally came. I was an adult, and I could get as far away from my family as I possibly could, but first, I felt that I had some situations to confront and try to resolve. I felt I needed to confront the people who hurt me. My mother and I tried several times to mend things. I went to live with her for a while. We argued all the time. She would tell me for hours everything she possibly thought of that was wrong with me, and I would rant and rave for hours for how stupid and irresponsible she was to abandon her children. When we both were tired of all the fighting, my mom would then tell me the fighting was actually beneficial for the both of us. We would then sit down, drink coffee, and play Scrabble. We even argued while we played the game.

We would get a manicure and pedicure together, and some days, we would spend laughing and crying together. I think we had to depart when we argued to the point where I threw my coffee in her face and called her names. Instantly, I ran and locked myself in her room. It did not help because she chopped the door in with a hammer. I was so scared. I was yelling, "Please do not hurt me, Momma!"

I knew this was it. I knew when she got in the door she was going to kick my behind. As she beat the door in, I was preparing myself for a boxing match. I actually knew I could not hit her, but I had to prevent her from bashing me in the head with that hammer.

All I kept hearing her say was how she was going to hurt me, of course, in a much more intimidating phrase. In came the door, and there she was standing there with a wet and sticky face. She was so angry with me, but she did not lay a hand on me. We both knew it was time for us to separate and take a break.

I left my mother's and went back to my father's where I prepared for my journey to Atlanta. I also confronted both of my uncles. They were both at my grandmother's house. I explained to them that they violated me. When I asked them why, one of them said, "You're lying, Melissa."

The other one became very hostile, and said, "I am going to slice your throat if you do not stop lying."

I knew, and they both knew I was telling the truth.

I was not taking any baggage with me to Atlanta (at least that was what I thought). Fighting with my mother, confronting my uncles, and having a made up mind to let the past go, was the first step towards my healing. I was actually tired of being angry. I was tired of holding grudges against my parents. I was tired of being mad at the whole world because of my past. My mind and my spirit were both exhausted. I got sick of blaming everyone for my troubled past. I wanted a new life. I wanted to find out who Melissa actually was. I wanted to be free from the bondage of not forgiving. I was ready for change. I was ready to forgive, move on, and try to enjoy the rest of my days on the earth.

As the years passed on, I came to the understanding that my mother was ill. She was battling a drug addiction along with posttraumatic stress syndrome. She could not keep me. She was not capable. My mother also explained to me that because all the years of physical and mental abuse she suffered from her second husband, we were better off where she left us in spite of our situation. I did not know that my mother suffered every day I suffered. I did not know her ex-husband severely beat her each time she mentioned our names. He told her she could not see her nigger children and tormented her for asking. I did not know that she was addicted to drugs. I did not know she was in and out of mental institutions while she was separated from us. I had no clue that she had nervous breakdowns because of the choices she made in her life.

When I analyzed all this, I could then forgive my mom, because I realized that she too is only human and she too is entitled to make mistakes. Most of all I realized and accepted that she was mentally ill. I have forgiven my mother, and I am able to love her in spite of her mistakes. Because I have forgiven my mom, my abusers, my father, and everyone who hurt me, I have been able to move on with my life in love and trust that brighter days are ahead.

If you are withholding forgiveness from someone, let me encourage you to go to that person and talk it out, argue it out, or work it out. Do what you have to do to set your spirit free. If you cannot forgive others, remember your heavenly father cannot forgive you. No, you do not have to like or accept what they have done to you, but you cannot go on the rest of your life harboring hatred and anger in your heart. This is called spiritual poison and is very deadly to the human spirit. If you cannot forgive others, remember you cannot blossom into who you were created to be. Having an unforgiving spirit will definitely paralyze you.

"Do you want to be made well?" Remember when Jesus asked the paralyzed man that question? Let me ask you the same question. Do you want to be made well? The first step to spiritual wellness is the cleansing of forgiveness towards others and yourself. If you really want to be made well you must master forgiveness. I know it's hard to forgive and love people when they, in your mind, ruin your life or rob you of your innocence. You must forgive them. You do not have to become best friends with your offenders, but you are required to forgive them. When they make promises they do not keep, forgive them. When they all of a sudden decide from out of nowhere, they want a divorce, I know this is a tough one, but forgive them anyway. When they have adulterous affairs, forgive them. When they smile in your face, but talk behind your back, smile, give them a hug, but most of all forgive them. When they tell malicious lies about you and slander your name say something kind to them and to someone else about them, and then forgive them. When they fire you from your job without a reason keep your cool, and forgive them. Do not go buy a shotgun and take everyone out of his or her misery.

Let me share this thought with you, I know you probably have not viewed things from this point. Look at your situation this way. People, like you, are only made of dirt. What do you expect them to do? Love you and treat you like God? No one can do that job better then the master of love himself. People are put here on earth to live, learn, and forgive just as you were put here to do. You will go nuts if you try to figure out why people do the things they do. They just do.

I believe if they truly knew why they did whatever they did to hurt you, they would have sense enough to sit down and tell you all about it. The truth is they haven't got a clue about why they behave the way they do. If they did, I am sure when they figure things out, they would come back to you and ask you to forgive them, but if they do not you just do your part- forgive. Forgive, live, and move on. It's called the game of life. I know with out a doubt that you are definitely playing the game, however I end this commentary by asking you this question. Are you winning by your acts of forgiveness or are you losing because you are not able to forgive?

Speak these words of forgiveness into your life today.

Today, I forgive (person's name) for violating me. I forgive you for hurting me. I forgive you for taking my kindness for granted. I forgive you for all the wrong things you may have said or done to hurt me. I forgive you for lying to me on several occasions. I forgive you for abusing me. I forgive you for making promises that you cannot keep. I forgive you for every time you made me cry. I forgive you for everything you ever done to me. I am free now because I have forgiven you. I am whole now because I have forgiven you. I can move on with my life now because I have forgiven you. I can love again because I have forgiven you. I can feel free to trust again because I have forgiven you. I know now that because I have forgiven you, my Father in Heaven now can begin to forgive me for all of the wrong I have done. And as forgiveness is in Him, it is in me because we are one together. Him in I, and I in Him. In Jesus' name, it is done.

19. Affirmation of Patience

That we be not slothful, but followers of them who through faith and patience inherit the promises (Hebrews 6: 12).

Someone asked me some time ago, "Why did God want us to learn patience?"

I explained to her that God has certain events planned for our lives that must take place at certain times. If we do not learn how to be patient, we could miss what He has for us. Now that I have had more time to think about the question that she asked me, I understand that the answer I gave her was somewhat true, but not complete.

Every human being must learn to practice patience. Why, because patience like love, peace, joy, and kindness are all fruits of the spirit. We must understand the soul is what gains eternal life, not the flesh. Impatience is a work of the flesh. Our flesh desires to satisfy itself with the things that our natural eyes can see. Most of us at some point have acted out of impatience to satisfy our flesh. We all have made some choices in our lives that later we were not too pleased with the results. The flesh wants what it wants, when it wants it, and will often provoke us to fill that which we desire without giving too much thought about long-term possible consequences. In order to see the promises of God manifest in our lives, we must learn to wait on the Lord with patience.

I know from experience that an impatient spirit will cause you much grief, much anxiety, and sometimes a loss. When we have an impatient spirit, we tend to say and do things that will delay the promises for our lives. I was so impatient I actually believed that I had to help the Lord bring His promises to pass in my life. I thought that once I prayed and received an approval from the Lord, everything else was in my hands. I would go around saying and doing things that I had no business whatsoever saying or doing. Many times my impatient spirit caused me to be embarrassed. I became impatient with the Lord. I would accuse Him of tricking me. I would stay up half of the night crying and asking God why He tricked me. I wore myself down trying to do what God could only do.

After several disappointments due to my lack of patience, I finally asked God to deliver me from the pride in my spirit that was causing me to think He needed me to control circumstances I had no power over and from the spirit of pride that led me to believe that I was in control. I finally surrendered and let God be in control. When I did this, I felt so much better. I told the Lord that since I could not be in control and speed up the process of my life, I would now harass Him with my fervent prayer. I made up in my mind that I would no longer go around trying to make things happen. I decided to stay out of God's business. I decided to let God make them happen. All I would do is just pray, pray, and pray some more. I prayed that God would help me to learn how to surrender my fears to Him. I finally realized that if God could not make what I desired happen then it was not meant to happen. And that was it for me.

In life, we must come to the understanding that God is in total control of our lives. We have to make an effort, but we do not control the outcome of our situations, God does. The truth is, the outcome of our situations has already been finished. God has already set everything in motion. He knows exactly everything that is to happen in your circumstances. You do not. You do not know what the end is going to be. You must use your faith to surrender, trust, and believe that everything will work out for your own good. If you trust God, your outcome will be one that is pleasing. If you wait on God, to bring what He has promised you to pass, you will never be disappointed. If you surrender all your fear, anxiety, and doubts to His bosom with heartfelt prayers, God will hear you and give you the kind of peace that will guard your mind and your heart and allow you to have rest.

You may be thinking, I do not know how to trust God, wait on God, and surrender to God. To trust Him is to believe His word. Trust that all that is in His word will prove to be true in due time (see Affirmation of Trust).

To wait on God means to be still long enough to see His promises fulfilled. When you're waiting on God, you have to sit still, be still, and still your mind. I had to learn this the hard way. I would pray and receive an answer from God, but then after some time had gone by and the promise had not happened, I would become frustrated, angry, and impatient, and I would run from the left to the right. I kept on running and running. What was I running from? My own impatient dysfunctional self. If you cannot sit still enough and wait for the Lord to bring what it is you want to pass, then you will never have what it is you want.

Creflo Dollar told us once that if we would be willing to wait forever for the promises of God to happen in our lives, then it would not be forever. I believe he was teaching me that I must be willing to wait forever on God if I had to. Pastor Dollar was right. God's promises do seem to take forever to happen, but it does not take God forever to bring a promise to pass. If that were the case then no one would be around to testify to others about the promises God has fulfilled in their lives. However, we must be at least willing to wait forever on God.

We release that which already belongs to Him from our hands into His hands. We are trusting that He knows best. We believe that He will work things out. Surrender is a very difficult job. Honestly, I do not enjoy surrendering things that matter most to me into God's hands who has the right to take that which is precious to me away from me. I do not enjoy releasing things over to someone who I cannot see. I do not enjoy waiting and waiting and waiting on God, but because I love Him and I wholeheartedly want to please Him, I surrender, I release, I wait, but most of all I trust that all that I turn over to Him, He will take care of dearly and give me what He thinks is best for me.

We must learn to understand that each lesson we learn and every trial and tribulation we experience, is somehow teaching us patience. For God is a spirit and we must worship him in spirit and in truth. Rick Warren explains in the *Purpose Driven Life*, that a heart of surrender is a heart of worship. When we surrender to God, we are worshiping Him in a beautiful way.

Developing your patience will help you here on earth. Many people are actually dead today because of lack of patience. Some have suffered severe tragedy and unnecessary pain because they could not wait on God. We must learn to bear the fruit of patience in our lives. When we learn patience, we are preparing for eternal life.

The bible clearly tells us that we must learn to be patient. It teaches us that through patience and faith we will inherit the promises of God. If we want to see God's promises happen in our lives then we must learn to develop a patient spirit.

Speak these words of patience into your life today.

Today, I will be patient with myself and with others. Today, I will wait on the promises of God to happen. Today, I will wait as long as I need to wait on the Lord, even if it takes forever. I am now developing a patient spirit by exercising patience in all that I do, all that I say, and all that I think. I am patient because God is patient. Today, I surrender; today, I trust; today, I wait; and today, I expect what God promises me to prove true. Because God is patient with me, I will be patient with God and others. In Jesus' name, it is done.

20. Affirmation to Defeat Fear

Fear not, little flock, for it is your Father's good pleasure to give you the kingdom (Luke 12:32).

Fear is a negative emotion that is a spiritual growth inhibitor. We want to be all that God wants us to be, but fear, the spiritual inhibitor, keeps the windows of heaven from opening, thus preventing our deepest desires from manifesting in our lives. Fear is a form of spiritual blockage. When we live our lives in constant fear, we discount the courage that God gives to us to complete certain assignments in our lives.

Have you allowed fear to stop you from achieving God's goals for you life? There was a time in my life when fear ruled my mind. I became consumed with the out come of my life and each situation that I found myself in. I would become so afraid I would break down and cry. I was so scared that everyone was going to hurt me as my mother did. I feared being abandoned over and over again. As a child I built an imaginary fort around my heart so that no one would ever make me feel the pain that my heart felt when my mother abandoned me. As I began to experience life, I did try to mentally tear the fort down, but I was too afraid to. Every time I thought I loved someone, I ended up hurt. In my mind I believed people would either hurt me, abandon me, or reject me. Now that I think about it, it is of no surprise that the very things I feared ended up becoming a reality. I was rejected, hurt, and abandoned. Experiencing these negative emotions over and over again almost drove me over the edge. My fears consumed me so, that I began to shut down mentally. I began to live a life of solitude just so I could avoid being hurt. I avoided several friendships and relationships so that I would not have to experience those negative emotions.

As I matured in Christ, I began to understand that because He rescued me, there was no need to be all by myself anymore. I realized that I could face all of my fears because He was a part of my life. I began to understand that with Jesus right by my side, I could begin to live and try to love again. As my relationship developed with the Lord, I soon noticed that the fear was subsiding. God designed different experiences that helped me overcome all of my fears. I began to do the very things I was always afraid of doing. I began to say all the things that I at one time would not dream of telling anyone. I soon learned that I overcame my fears by facing them one by one. I looked my hurts right in their face and I told them that instead of them causing me to have fear, they would one day help me minister to someone. I looked abandonment in the eyes and told it that it could not follow me around any longer. I told the spirit of rejection that Jesus Christ loves me and accepts me and that His love was enough. Of course the devil tried to tell me otherwise, but I cast him out of my mind each and every time he attacked me. I would scream out loud, "You are a liar, Satan, and there is no truth in you. For I am loved and accepted by God!"

I would then start shouting and singing praises to God. I thanked Him for delivering me from such feelings. It was tough, but I can honestly say that today I will just about say and do anything that I believe the spirit of God is leading me to do. I do so with no fear. I speak my mind, I share my feelings, and I face all of the emotions that surface in my life.

Do what it is you are afraid of doing. Do not focus on what the end will be. Just keep your mind set on fulfilling your purpose here on earth. When you become afraid, just remember God is with you and for you. When you become afraid, cast it down with the power of your words. When you begin to do what is in your heart and live your life, there can not be any room for fear. Fear is a normal negative emotion, but you can stop it in its tracks when it attacks you.

113

A special word from God (As I finished writing this commentary my spirit uttered these words, and I wrote them exactly as I heard with my spiritual ears).

Be ye not afraid my dear child for the Lord thy God is with thee on thy right side; for the Lord thy God is with thee on thy left side; for the Lord thy God is behind thee; for the Lord thy God is in front of thee; for the Lord thy God is all around thee. From my presence, no man can escape, for I am that presence. I am all that there is. I am all that you are. I am all that you will ever be. I am He who rides the north, east, west, and south winds. I am He who is fearless. I am and so too are you. Be ye fearless! Says the Lord God Almighty.

Speak to the fear that Inhibits your spiritual growth:

Fear, I am now taking time to acknowledge you. I must tell you it is now time for you to go away. Fear, I face you each time I get ready to step out in faith and live my dreams. You seem to hold me back. Well not this time. You must move out of my way. For you are causing spiritual blockage in my life, and this is not good. So many opportunities have come, but because of you, I have missed out. Love has come, but you chased it away. Why, because I let you. Well not any more. Opportunities for prosperity have come, but you seized it instead of me. Why, because I allowed you to. God did not give me the spirit of fear; He gave me a spirit of love and a sound mind. Fear it is time for me to dismiss you out of my life, my mind, and my spirit. Now that I have acknowledged you and have faced you, I command you by the power of my words to BE GONE! In the name of Jesus Christ of Nazareth. I am walking into my destiny fearless; I am reclaiming all that has been lost due to your toxicity. I am fearless, and I am now free! Good-bye fear, I am no longer your dwelling place. In Jesus' name, it is done!

21. Affirmation Love

Love bears all things believes all things, hopes in all things, and endures all things. Love never fails (1 Corinthians 13:7).

We all have our own ideas and definition for this powerful four-letter word. Some have experienced love from the ministry of marriage, while others may have experienced love taking care of animals. Some have chosen to experience love through their higher power. It really does not matter how you experience love, but it is important that you experience love in your life. The truth is we all need love to thrive. It has been said that babies born premature survive through the loving strokes of a warm hand caressing their fragile bodies while they struggle for their lives. Love is a feeling that all living things must have. Without love, people grow cold and drift away. I chose to find true love through Him who created me. All of my life, I looked for love from my mother, but I did not get it. I looked for love from my father, but it was not there either. I looked for love from different men, but they had nothing for me. It was when I looked to God, love began to manifest itself into my life.

As a little girl, I felt unloved. I was deeply hurt that my mother abandoned me. My father did not allow himself to love me the way a father should love his daughter. He loved me the best way he knew how, but I needed showers of love because of the hurt my mother caused me. My dad was not an emotional person. I was not loved by any of my children's fathers. I was hurt because I believed that no one could love me. As I grew closer to God, I learned the true meaning of love. I have concluded that to love is a conscious decision that we make up in our minds and our hearts to do. We either choose to allow love to grow within us or we make the decision to allow hate and resentment to grow within us. The two cannot reside within a person. You will either harbor love inside of you or you will harbor hate. The choice is yours to make.

I wanted to be loved by people, but they could not love me. Why, because I could not love me. I asked God to teach me about love. The very first thing He taught me was that the love I so desperately craved was buried deep within my soul, underneath all my fears, hurts, and pains. I needed to work through all of my disturbed childhood emotions so that love would be able to flow throughout my whole being. I remember thinking that if God was good then there had to be some good somewhere within me because I looked like Him. I also realized that love already existed somewhere within me, because I was connected to love (God).

Becoming aware of the fact that I looked like God was the first and most important lesson I learned about love. Love began with knowing God and knowing me. I became aware that if I wanted someone to love me then I had to be that which I desired. I desired to be loved. Therefore, I took on the challenge of becoming love myself. I say it was a challenge for me because I knew nothing about it. I, like many other people, was confused about love. I thought that I was receiving love if I had sex with a man. I know now that I knew nothing about love.

If you are like me, you may have spent a lot of energy looking to others to make you feel loved, or searching for love from people who cannot and will not love you. In my search for love, I never knew it was always right there with me. I never knew it was just an affirmation away. I did not have a clue that all the love that I so desperately craved from another was inside of me, waiting to spring forth. In my decision to become that which I desired the most, by grace, the Holy Spirit revealed to me that the seed of love had been planted inside of me while developing in my mother's womb. I was informed that it was my responsibility to nourish and develop this precious seed within me.

I again was so thrilled and felt honored to finally be tuning in with God. I was actually hearing form God, how exciting! I was willing to experience whatever it took to become love. I remember reading a book once that stated I would attract exactly what I was. So here I was, twenty-five years old, and ready to discover something so beautiful, that for the most part of my life I thought was far from my reach, only to realize that all the love I was seeking was right there in my soul. At the age of twenty-five, I discovered that I was the love I craved for all my life. I discovered that the seed of love was put in me, but was suppressed due to the negative experiences I had in my childhood. The seed of love that God planted in me was not nourished properly as a child. However, I came to know that just because my mother did not nourish the seed of love inside me did not mean that it was not there.

Each of us has the seed of love within us. If we nourish it, it can begin to grow. It is important that we learn how to nourish it. When something is nourished, it then begins to grow. I learned to water my seed with the truth. I realized that in love there is only truth and no deception. Therefore, I began to tell the truth about my feelings. I began to share what I believed to be true with others. Finally, my soul awakened to the truth about love. Somehow, the seed that had been suppressed began to spring up with new life. I began to feel love growing inside of me. All of the resentment, hate, hurt, and pains of my past began to be replaced with overwhelming feelings of love. Sharing my truth with others, telling myself the truth, and finding out the truth about God allowed my seed of love to begin to sprout. We must learn to be honest with ourselves and with others.

I had to learn and I am still learning to be patient. We must nourish our seed of love by being patient with ourselves and others (see commentary on patience). I had to understand that if I was to be love, I had to keep on practicing patience with myself and with others. Practicing patience has been a challenging skill for me to master. I remember there were days when I awoke and had to tell the Lord, "Oh, Jesus, I did it again, please forgive me."

I also remember days when I would write in my journal, *Lord, I do not understand why I keep doing what I am doing over and over again.*

There were days when I felt so sad because I felt like I could not do anything right. I realize that years have passed and I have improved in some areas in my life. I am still making improvements on others. Please let me encourage you to be patient with yourself. It is okay to make mistakes. That is why the bible encourages us to work out our salvation. God knows this process is not easy. To be quite honest, many times I have felt like a basket case trying to work out my salvation. Believe me, I have done everything I could possibly think of to become love. Guess what? All those things that I thought of actually worked! So, if you desire to experience love, do whatever it takes to discover the love within you.

Love also requires that we be patient with others. I know this is tough, but when you can learn to be patient with other people, you are well on your way to experiencing love.

We must learn to place ourselves in a position of humility. Love is not proud. Many people fall short here. I have discovered that true love walks in humility on all occasions. When we walk in the spirit of love, we are walking constantly in humility. Pure love has no desire to be proud; it actually takes delight in humbling itself before others. I love to practice humility because I have discovered that God takes delight in us when we present ourselves as little children in his presence. I desired to become humble. I did not really know how to be humble. I believe it came over me when I realized how my life could have easily been destroyed through the choices I made in the past. Realizing this made me just desire to be low in the presence of God. Just realizing that because of my past, I could have been mentally insane, strung out on drugs, or even a prostitute, but instead God chose me to rise above my circumstances and soar as an eagle flying across the sky. He chose to give me a second chance. This brought me into humility.

If you are one who struggles with a proud spirit, let me encourage you to meditate on where God has brought you. Really think about it. I am almost sure if you focus, you too will become a more humble person. If you are one who has a proud heart and have nothing to meditate on because you do not think God has brought you from anywhere, then know this: (spirit speaks) *"I create all flesh. I create all life. I created you. Be ye therefore humble. Know that I create each day a new day. Know this, I do not have to call another day forth, because another day does not exist unless I speak it into being. Be ye clothed in humility knowing that I am watching to see that your heart beats intact with motion, for it is my love that allows thy heart to beat rhythmically. Be ye humble in knowing that I am is the air you are breathing. Be humble in recognizing that I chose to share my breath with thee because of love. So you too love as I have loved thee."*

Humility pleases the lord. We must also nourish the seed of love with kindness. What does it mean to be kind? We show kindness through our words and actions. Say kind things to yourself and to others. Be kindness. How? Do kind things for yourself and for others. There are several ways to be kind. Send a thank you card to some one who has been kind to you. Have lunch with a homeless person; I bet that would really brighten their day. Buy some bread and crackers, hang out at the zoo, and feed the birds. Did you know that God uses us as avenues of provision to see to it that his precious birds eat every day? I bet you did not know that the birds know this as well. Is that not love?

Being kind is important to God and should be important to us as well. We can nourish the seed of love within us by being slow to anger. We do not need to get mad and upset at every little thing. I know there will be times in our lives that we become angry and this is a natural feeling, however if we become angry quickly and easily then we are not practicing love. We must not become angry with ourselves because we make mistakes. It is okay to make mistakes because we can learn valuable lessons from them. Please stop being angry with others when they make mistakes. Continue to love them. Try to understand that somehow through their mistakes, they will learn to practice love towards you or someone else in a more experienced manner.

We must also nourish our seed with protection. Protection is important in learning to love. When we learn to love, we learn to protect those we love. We protect each other by covering one another. We protect their feelings by being mindful of the things that we say to them. This is an area in my life that I make special efforts to master. I know we call it being honest and speaking the truth in love; however, if we are to learn how to love as God loves, we must watch what we say to people. Before we just blurt out things, we must first stop and think, how will what we have to say make the other person feel. Love always protects. It protects others' feelings. I love and will protect my children. I make sure at all times they are in a safe environment. I protect them. In what ways have you protected those whom you love?

Love covers a multitude of sins. We must learn to cover one another. How? The first step is to stop judging people. We must love people in spite of their behavior. This does not mean that we have to accept abuse or neglect, but we must not look down on others because of the things they do. You do not know why they are doing what they are doing, but it is your responsibility as a person, walking in love, to trust that in spite of all their actions God is also preparing and teaching them lessons as well. How do we continue even though we have been hurt by others? How do we press on when our trust has been violated time after time? How can we go on when the only thing we have ever experienced is sadness, hurt, and pain? How does a mother survive when she is overwhelmed in grief due to the loss of her child? How do we continue when we have lost our job, our home, and our family? How do young women survive due to the mental trauma of incest, and rape?

Whether we realize it or not, we survive through difficult circumstances because of the seed of love that lives within us. There is so much love planted on the inside of us, but we as human beings must bring it out. As a young woman, I have concluded that no one can ever love you the way that God loves you. I have also learned that we must love even when we are not loved. I encourage you to nourish the seed of love within yourself. Look to God to love you, not man.

Because man will let you down, but God will never fail you. Keep on loving. Love at all times; learn to love the experience of life. Thank God that you have a heart that chooses to love, and if you do not, then affirm today that you have a heart that chooses to love. Trust that every experience you ever have allows you the opportunity to learn the great lesson of love. And remember:

Spirit Speaks:

Love is the greatest commandment; love is all that you are. Love is the key to pass into eternity; love is the promise of your future. Love is the higher power to whom which you believe. Love is God and God is love. Love is what awakes you each day. Love is what has helped you through each trial and tribulation you have gone through. Yes, you may have gone through the fire, but only to come forth as pure gold, and you have gone through to come out to manifest thyself as a higher form of love. Love is the key to hope, and success. Choose to love instead of hurt, choose love instead of growing cold, choose to love rather than give up, choose to love rather than fall away, choose to love rather than hate. Choose the most important thing and that is love.

Speak these words of love into your life today.

I am an expression of love. My words, thoughts, and actions shall be expressed as love. I choose to love in spite of my past hurts and pains. I am nourishing the seed of love within myself by being all that there is in love to be. I love all that God has placed into my care. I love the gift of life that has been imparted unto me. I love the essence of who I am. And I love the truth that is being revealed to me this day, which is that I am created to represent all that love is. In Jesus' name it is done.

22. Affirmation Purpose

And we know that all things work together for good to them that love God, to them who are the called according to His purpose (Romans 8:28).

Have you ever asked yourself the questions, "What am I alive for? Why did I come into this world?"

The answers to your questions are simple, yet some make them very difficult. There are many reasons for your being alive. One reason God allowed you the precious gift of life is because He knew that by you being here the world would become a better place. He gave you special talents to share with the world to touch the lives of others. He gave you precious gifts to use to bring light into the world. Jesus is the light of the world. Do you remember the scripture where Jesus says, "You are the light of the world"? Well, you actually are. Jesus also commanded that we let our light shine before men so that they may see our good works and glorify our father in heaven. You see you are an important asset to this planet. That is why it is so important for you to discover exactly what gifts God has imparted into you to share with the world. Yes, you were actually created to keep the world going around.

What talents has God blessed you with that you can use to bless others around you? Please use them, because if you do not then the Holy Spirit becomes grieved. It saddens the heart of God when we do not use all the talents that He gives us. In the eyes of God, our life is just a waste when we do not share what He has given us with the world. Do you know why? Because when we share the talents that

God gives to us, we are actually sharing a special part of God with the world. That special part is the force of his creativity. We are actually expressing a piece of God when we write music, sing songs, preach the gospel, invent things, practice medicine, or teach others. Know that you were created to express the God in you through your talents.

Another reason God created you is to teach you valuable lessons that will assist you in the afterlife. The afterlife is a spiritual journey that each one of us must take at our own appointed time. God would have us consider life as a special moment. God considers a moment a very short time. In this moment that we have here on earth, God wants us to learn lessons that will benefit us when we take our journey into eternity.

I believe the greatest lesson that God wants us to learn is the lesson of love. Have you noticed that throughout all your circumstances that you have faced in life, whether they are difficult trials or simple tests to pass, that you can always link them to love? I believe that there is so much love in the eternal life promised to us that God ordained it the greatest commandment. I like to believe we must learn the true meaning of love in order to see God. If we do not we cannot be with God in the afterlife. Now would be a good time to take self inventory on all of your present and past circumstances and ask yourself these questions: How has this situation taught me to love more? Have I learned to love more by this experience? Have I expressed the piece of God inside of me by using the gifts He gave me to add light into this world?

To share your light with the world and to learn lessons to prepare you for eternal life, are some of the reasons why you were so carefully knitted together in your mother's womb. Learn to share your light today by affirming purpose into your life with your own mouth!

Speak these words of purpose into your life today!

Great and almighty God, I will now allow the part of you that has so long desired to be expressed through the talents you have given me to spring forth. I know now that for this reason, I was created. I will now use all the talents you have given me to help make this world a better place. For this is my purpose. I will share my light with men so that they can glorify you. For this purpose, I was created. I will so carefully learn all the lessons that you designed to prepare me for eternity. For this purpose, I was created. I will master the greatest lesson to be learned, and that is the lesson of unconditional love. I will love all people, and every good thing that represents you. For this purpose, I was created. For in this day, there is purpose. For in yesterday, there was purpose. For in my future, there is purpose. For in my heart, there is purpose. For in you, there is purpose. For in eternal life, there is purpose. Thank you Great Spirit for purpose. In Jesus' name it is done!

23. Affirmation Intuitive Insight (Discernment)

"When you follow the leading of your spirit, you can never be mislead" (MJ).

This is a very special affirmation. Intuitive insight is the greatest power designed into every living thing. It is somewhat similar to the gift of the Holy Spirit, but different. The thing that distinguishes the two is that the Holy Spirit is a real person and intuitive insight is within each and every thing that breathes. Intuitive insight is a part of every living creature, from humans to animals, even insects. When we are filled with the Holy Spirit, our intuitive insight becomes more heightened and we are more receptive to being led by the Holy Spirit. However, what about those who do not believe in a higher power? Are they left without guidance? Of course not! You see God loved us enough to equip us with everything that we would need to keep us from harm and unseen dangers. Intuitive insight is a certain knowing that comes from within our spirit. Have you ever had a certain feeling that you should take a different route home than your normal way of traveling? Maybe later you discovered that there was an accident, and you were glad that you followed your instincts. Or, you had a certain feeling that you should call a friend or a loved one, and when you did, they have been sick or just have been thinking of you. All of these experiences are part of your intuitive insight. The power of intuitive insight depends upon each individual.

Remember intuitive insight is not the Holy Spirit. The Holy Spirit is himself a person, but intuitive insight is naturally designed into the human spirit. The presence of the Holy Spirit is a spiritual activator to bring your intuitive insight into its full awareness. The Holy Spirit's responsibility is to bring you into alignment with the will of God, to teach you, and tell you all things that are to come. God did not design us to wander around lost. He deeply desires us to rely on our intuitive insight and the Holy Spirit for direction.

There have been times when I felt led to do certain things, and because I followed my intuition, I was blessed. For instance, there was a time when I worked as a waitress at the Waffle House. My car was repossessed, and I decided I would work part time to save to buy another car. On my first night, I reported to work about nine thirty on a Friday evening and began to wait on the customers. I was very tired because I had already worked my regular shift. I had no business trying to work another ten-hour shift.

I remember it was about two thirty in the morning, and I went to the back to put some lip gloss on my lips. When I looked in the mirror, I saw how worn out and tired I was. I also felt in my spirit that I should go home. I asked the manager if she would be upset with me if I went home. She asked me if the crew that night had offended me in any way. I told her no and explained that I felt in my spirit that I needed to be at home resting. I also told her that I lost my car and was trying to save a little extra money but I felt like God wanted to work my situation out instead of me working it out. I also informed her that I had to be obedient to the things I was feeling. She then took me home.

When I got home that night I told God I was not going to interfere with anything that He was trying to do in my life. I promised Him that I would wait as long as it took Him to work out my transportation situation. When I decided to let God be in control of my situation, He performed a miracle for me. About one month later, a man and his wife blessed me with a dependable car. I never returned to get the hourly wages I earned that evening waiting tables. One week, we were running low on groceries, and I arose early in the morning to pray. I asked God to make a provision so we could buy groceries.

126

When I opened my bible for my morning study, my eyes landed on a passage that read, *I am the Lord God who performs miracles.* I then thanked God for providing provision. That same morning, I was on my way to work, and I felt led to go back to the Waffle House and asked for the money I earned that one night. It was to total about thirteen dollars.

When I arrived, I asked to speak with the manager and a man came out. I was expecting to see the lady who hired me, but she was off that morning. I explained to the man that I never received my hourly pay. He searched the system and could not find my name anywhere in the computer. He asked me why I quit on my first night, and I explained that I had to listen to my spirit. He then began to testify that God saved him from losing his home. He then informed me that I was not in the system. As I began to head out the door, he reached in his back pocket, pulled out his wallet, and gave me all that was in it. He said, "I know you need this."

I was so happy. I thanked the man and I began praising God all the way to work. God did not let me and my children go hungry. He answered my prayer. This special miracle touched my heart. I do not know who the man was, but he blessed us with grocery money. I sum it all up to following my intuition. If I had not went home the evening that my spirit led me to, I might not have been blessed with a car. If I had not followed my intuition and stopped by the Waffle House as my spirit led me to do, then I would not have received my blessings. It is best to always follow your intuition. Your human spirit will never lead you astray. When you become filled with the presence of the Holy Spirit, your intuitive insight is heightened. You become more sensitive to the leading of your spirit.

Several people have not yet mastered the ability to follow the leading of their intuitive insight. This is due to the spiritual inhibitor fear. It is crucial to be rid of fear (see affirmation to defeat fear). Fear will keep you from following the leading of your spirit, which could possibly prevent beautiful things from happening in your life. Jesus himself was a follower of his intuitive insight. Although He was full of the Spirit, there were times when He was aware of people's thoughts, and He knew when to withdraw himself from the crowds to rest or avoid danger. Jesus was led by His intuitive insight, which was heightened by the presence of the Holy Spirit. Jesus was human flesh just as we are; however, Jesus knew to rely on the leading of His spirit.

In the book of Matthew, beginning at the fourth chapter, it says: *Then Jesus was led by the Spirit into the desert to be tempted by the devil.* He was aware that the time was near for His ministry to begin, so He prepared Himself for the work that God sent Him to do.

Never second guess your spirit. If the Holy Spirit has not filled you, ask God to fill you with the Holy Spirit so that your natural intuitive insight deepens. Every living creature has natural instincts whether they believe in God or not, but knowing God and being filled with the Holy Spirit brings those natural instincts to a higher level so that you can become aware of all things. Do not be discouraged if you think you are not filled with the Holy Spirit. All you have to do is ask God to fill you, and He will. Begin to become aware of your natural intuitive instincts, and as you grow in your faith, ask God to fill you with the Holy Spirit.

Awaken the gift of intuitive insight inside of you today!

I am now relying on my intuition to lead and guide me. The presence of the Holy Spirit now fills me to stimulate my intuitive insight. I know when to speak, when to quiet my soul, and when to take necessary actions. I know that I am created for a specific assignment. How do I know this? Because my spirit tells me so. I know that I am accomplishing great things through the leading of my intuition. From this day on, I shall listen to my intuitive insight at all times. In Jesus' name, it is done!

24. Affirmation of Receiving

That the blessing of Abraham might come on the gentiles through Jesus Christ; that we might receive the promise of the Spirit through faith (Galatians 3:14) .

Did you know that it is so important that we learn how to receive? So many people have not learned how to receive. Some of us can't even receive a compliment. When you are not able to receive, you are spiritually blocked. You could be serving God faithfully, or be a naturally good person; however, if you do not learn to receive, you are spiritually congested. God has so many great blessings for us, and He wants us to receive them. Fear, doubt, confusion, disobedience, and our lack of ability to receive are what stop us from His blessings. Just as there is the spiritual law of giving, there is the spiritual law of receiving.

I remember going to church where they always taught me to give. I actually do not remember anyone teaching me to receive. Different preachers would say God wants us to be givers, but never one time did I hear them say God wants you to receive. They said God would bless me, which indeed was true. Exactly how would God bless me? I now know through spiritual maturity that God would indeed bless me, but He wanted me to be able to receive my blessings.

There is more to the blessing than being able to pay all the bills and having enough to eat. Yes, these are all blessings. It is a blessing to wake up another day and to be in good health. We should count these all as blessings. God promised to take care of us each day. Jesus said we should not worry about food and clothing because God would provide. So many times in my life I would ask God to bless me. When He did, I used to tell myself I did not deserve to be blessed. I gave my life to Him. I was doing my very best to love and serve Him wholeheartedly. Why did I not deserve a blessing? It was all in my mind. My mind was not able to receive the blessings that God granted me. My mind was double. I would ask God to bless me but then I would tell Him I do not deserve it. Boy, was that type of thinking dysfunctional.

It is time for us to learn about the blessing of receiving. Have you ever felt like there was something that God wanted you to have, but for some reason you just could not seem to get it? Have you ever felt as though you were right on the verge of a breakthrough, but it was not coming? I know I have. This is because you lack the knowledge to receive.

Fear and past disappointments have congested the spiritual pathways in which God has chosen to get your blessings to you. This is why you cannot receive what you feel is rightfully yours. There are several steps to clear up this spiritual congestion. Understand that it is not a sin to expect to receive. If you are giving and saying, "I do not expect anything back," then you are not thinking properly. The law of giving goes hand in hand with the law of receiving. No, you should not expect anything back from who you are blessing, but you should expect to receive a blessing from God's storehouse because you are sowing into someone's life. We must expect to receive what it is we desire. Having a spirit of expectation sends signals to God that you are actually waiting on Him and expecting Him to do great things in your life, just as His word says we are to do. This puts you in a position to begin to receive.

We also must affirm receiving words from our mouths each day. In doing this, we actually speak the gifts of receiving into our lives. We must learn to speak to our minds. We need to begin to tell our minds that we are expecting to receive. Tell your mind that it is okay to receive blessings from the seeds you sow. If you do not expect anything, then chances are, you will not receive anything. This will help transform the way we think, which will decongest the spiritual blockage in our lives a great deal. We also must learn to believe that we are worth receiving God's blessings. Low self-esteem prevents us from receiving things God desires for us to have. Because we feel so unworthy, we do not believe we are worthy of blessings. We have to learn to convince our minds that, yes, it is okay to expect to receive. We must also stop living in fear. We need to stop being afraid to live our dreams. We need to stop being afraid of making mistakes.

Life is full of disappointments, and I have had my share. I chose to learn valuable lessons and press on towards the mark in my higher calling of Christ Jesus. I have had my heart broken, my feelings hurt, and I have had to deal with rejection and abandonment in my life. These difficult circumstances had me spiritually congested for most of my life. I made a decision to not allow these hurtful circumstances to stop me from experiencing God's goodness. I decided to believe God, trust my spirit, and never doubt God's ability to raise me up nor His power to help me be the mother I need to be for my children, and the woman I need to be for Him. I made a conscious choice to grow and to make the best of my situations. I chose to learn how to receive God's blessing of unmerited favor in my life by my acts of faith, courage, and obedience regardless of my past. I have chosen to learn how to receive miracles from heaven, however, they may come through my faith. I have chosen to receive the promise of a future in my walk with God. I have chosen to receive all that God promises for me. You too can make a conscious choice to learn to receive all the good that God has for you by simply conditioning your mind, heart, and spirit to receive God's harvest blessing for your life. For your blessings are waiting and they do have your name and your name only written upon them.

Speak these words of receiving into your life today!

I am receiving the full fledged promise of God. I am receiving every blessing that God ever intended for me to have. I am receiving every good thing that God has prepared for me. I am receiving miracles from heaven. I am receiving (begin to name all the things you want to receive one by one). I am receiving God's favor in my life. I am receiving God's blessing on which all that I lay my hands. I am receiving the blessing to do the things I was created to do. I am receiving my rightful place in eternity at the appointed time. I have a receiving mind, I have a receiving spirit, and I have receiving attitude. I am receiving, I am receiving, I am receiving, I am receiving, I am receiving, I am receiving all good things that have been ordained for me since the beginning of time! Therefore, so, I have spoken it and so it shall be. In Jesus' name, it is done!

25. Affirmation of Miracles

The God who does great things. Things that are unsearchable; marvelous things without number (Job 5:9).

So many of us long for miracles. We hear testimonies of miracles from others, but we have yet to experience a true miracle for ourselves. Are you the kind of person who has never experienced a miracle from God? Let's go deeper and define exactly what a miracle is. A miracle is a supernatural divine intervention propelled by the command of God.

My aunt once shared a miracle story she saw on a television program. The story touched a very special place in my heart. She told me that there was a woman who had two children, lived in an upstairs apartment, and had no one to share thanksgiving with or any food to eat. She had some hot dogs that she was going to feed the children. All of their hearts were sad. I can truly empathize with her, because I know what it is like not to be with your family around the holidays and have too little food for everyone. The woman prayed to the Lord. That evening, the woman went outside and down the stairs when an elderly woman invited her and her children to have Thanksgiving dinner with her. At first, the woman refused and said she did not want to intrude, but the old woman insisted and explained that she had prepared apple pies, stuffing, and other delicious foods. The woman finally accepted the invitation. The woman, the elderly lady, and the children ate together for Thanksgiving. They laughed, talked, and enjoyed each other's company all night long.

The next evening, the woman decided to go downstairs and thank the elderly lady for Thanksgiving dinner only to find that the apartment was vacant. She then spoke with the landlord and asked what happened to the woman and was informed that the apartment had been vacant for over three months. I love this beautiful miracle story because I know that the Lord heard the woman's prayer. God was so concerned that she and her children had a happy Thanksgiving that He commanded an angel to dine with her and the children. God felt her and her children's sadness and was moved by her prayer. She asked for a miracle, and she received one.

Several people have experienced miracles in their lives. Miracles come in many different ways. I once heard of a miracle in Africa. A minister died and had been dead for a few days. He and his wife were faithful followers of Jesus Christ. His wife would not and could not accept the fact that her husband had died. She continuously recited the word of God and believed that He would work a miracle. She did this constantly and diligently, even through the funeral. At the funeral, she kept speaking life into her husband, and suddenly he began to breathe again. This startled everyone at the service, and they began to praise God. I watched a video of his testimony and almost could not believe it myself. However, I remember the scripture that reads, *Is anything too hard for God?* (Genesis 18:14). *For with God nothing shall be impossible* (Luke 1:37). I then realized that I was no one to judge this man's testimony, and I assumed this to be yet another miracle.

When I was around fifteen years old, my pastor's daughter and her husband were expecting their first child. Everyone in our church was so excited about the baby's arrival. When the time came for the baby to be born, she was born dead. The doctors pronounced the baby's death. The pastor, her mother, and her husband kept on praying to the Lord. The baby was left in the room with them, and thirty minutes passed by. As they were praying, the baby began to move and cry. The doctors rushed in and began to assist the baby girl. They were all convinced that the baby would suffer severe brain damage and mental retardation. As the years passed, I watched the little girl grow, laugh, and play as any other child. This was yet another miracle.

There is a man in my church whose father became very ill. He is an elderly man very well in age who sincerely loves God. Although He is very old, I watch him get around as if he is still a young man. I have always admired that and each time I see him, I smile with deep joy. Whenever I would miss a church service he would always ask me where was I at. I would just smile a never say a word. I know God is truly with him. I enjoy listening to his long-winded speeches at church. As I listen, I sense a genuine spirit in Him. Well, he became so ill that he had to be hospitalized. The doctors did not expect a positive outcome, but his son did. I like to think his son was expecting a miracle. One morning while he was in the hospital, the doctors called his family at home to come because he was dying. His family came to the hospital and the doctors suggested that a minister be called to the room to console the family and pray the man into eternity. The son disagreed and said they would themselves pray as a family. I can only imagine the anguish that clenched the young man's heart as he watched his father take his last breaths. The young man and his father began to recite the twenty-third Psalm together. As they recited the passage, the young man became so overwhelmed in his soul that he fell on his knees and cried before the Lord asking God to spare his father's life because he felt as though there was still more work for them to do together. Guess what? That is just what God did. The man testified about this miracle and my soul became very glad. I know this was a true miracle. Whatever work they have to do together I am sure it is getting done.

Living a life of faith requires that we believe in miracles. We study in our bibles every day about the wondrous miracles that God performed then, yet currently we act as if He is not able to do the things He did thousands of years ago. When I read about the heroes of the bible, I have made some connections to all the miracles that God performed. The first connection is the connection of faith that the heroes of the bible had. They were connected to God by their faith. They believed that the God they served could do anything. What amazes me is that they also believed that even if God decided not to do a miracle, they would die believing that He could if He wanted to. Now that is faith.

Before the three Hebrew boys were thrown into the burning furnace, they affirmed to the king that they were not bowing down to any false Gods, even if it cost them their lives. They affirmed, "The God we serve is able to save us." In other words, they were affirming, "The God we serve is able to perform a miracle!"

I do not know how you feel, but if I were about to be tied up and thrown into hot blazing fires, I would definitely need God to perform a miracle. That is just what God did. Because they affirmed with their own words an affirmation of faith, a miracle was performed. The Hebrew boys were saved from the fiery furnace.

When the overshadowing of the power of the most high impregnated Mary, she conceived baby Jesus. When it was revealed to her that these things would happen, she affirmed, "May it be unto me as you have said." In others words, she said, "Let the miracle be just as you have stated." I know Mary knew this was a miracle because she had not even been with a man . So many women to this day have been told that they could never bear children and are deeply saddened by this. However I say to the barren woman that there is nothing that God cannot do.

We must learn to speak miracles into our lives every day. If we do not, then we will not see any. As I walk with God, I enjoy seeing Him perform miracles each day. I find it a miracle that my heart has been beating since I was twenty-one days old inside my mother's womb and has not missed one single beat since then. I find it a miracle to grow another life inside my womb and then have the strength to push the precious life from me into this world. I find it a miracle to inhale and exhale without remembering to do so. I find it a miracle to wake up each day, for I know that each new day does not have to exist. I have always been amazed that even though I am a single mother and face financial difficulties, God has always provided miracle money for the girls and me.

I remember, some time ago, it was my friend's birthday. I wanted him to have a special birthday. I had a twenty-five dollar gift certificate to Red Lobster, and I wanted to take him there. Of course, it costs more than twenty-five dollars to eat at Red Lobster. Therefore, I had to pay extra money I did not have. Payday was a few days away, and I spent my last to ensure that he had a happy birthday. I remember he said, "I know you do not have the extra money, Melissa," but I insisted I had it. I believed that God had enough in His storehouses in heaven to supply me with what I needed. I was not concerned about money. I enjoy seeing other people happy, and I believe everyone should celebrate the gift of life. I have always enjoyed giving gifts to others without expecting anything from them in return. I truly enjoy warming another's spirit with something special. Everyone deserves to feel like they are cared about.

We finished eating and were on our way to the car. From out of nowhere a twenty-dollar bill flew right to my feet. As I reached down to grab it, I surprisingly said, "Look! A twenty-dollar bill flew right at my feet!"

He said, "You see, Melissa, God knew you did not have the extra money to treat me to dinner so He gave it right back to you."

I was amazed, and I learned a good lesson from this experience. I learned that God sees your heart. When you give with good intentions, you always are blessed. I knew I did not have the money to spend over the gift certificate I had, but because I gave genuinely from my heart and believed that I had enough, God worked a miracle, small to some but great in my eyes. God's sees every good deed that we do.

I remember being short on cash, and I was experiencing financial difficulties, which is quite common in the life of a single mother. My transportation was repossessed, and I was really saddened by the whole experience. I had taken the girls to Mc Donald's for an ice cream cone. I figured ice cream would cheer us all up. I did not have the extra money, but after all the hardships we were suffering, I believed we all deserved ice cream. As we were coming home, crossing the street, Jasmine yelled, "Look, Mommy!"

I looked down and picked up a twenty-dollar bill. I smiled and told the Lord, "Thank you."

Twenty dollars may seem petty to many people, but it really helps when you are a single mother, struggling with two children by yourself and there is always just enough to get by.

I also remember God performed another financial miracle for me. I received my paycheck, and I paid all the bills. I did not tell anyone that I needed money, except God himself. I did not have much money left. I remember a co-worker that I worked with at the hospital said she had something for me. She handed me an envelope, which had one hundred dollars in it. I cried because she said, "God has instructed me to give you this."

There are so many other financial miracles that God has blessed me with. If I speak of them, they would be too many to tell! Just know that God has never failed to provide for my children and I, and He will never fail to provide for you.

So, believe me when I tell you that miracles are just an affirmation away. Would you like to begin to experience miracles today! Begin by affirming miracles each day. As you see them manifest, do not forget to count the small things as being great. As you do this, the miracles will get bigger and bigger. Make a faith connection with God. Decide in your mind that the creator of this universe can do anything. Believe in His infinite power. Rest assured that He is a God of miracles.

Spirit speaks:

Be confident in this: Those who believe that I am He who is able will see manifestations of God's miracles. I do as I please, and I am well pleased when those who claim to know me believe in my infinite power. I am the miracle which thou doest desire. Miracles are all in my hands as I pour them from the palms of my hand, they fall into the bosoms of those who have their hands lifted in prayer and believing that the things they so desire are being poured forth from my hands into their lives.

Ask God for miracles each day. Begin to focus on the miracles that you are surrounded with each day that you so easily take for granted. Expect to receive from the supernatural, heaven sent miracles. Remember affirming miracles are a gift of the spirit.

Affirm the gift of miracles into your surroundings today!

Today is yet another miracle! For, I am a miracle. Today, I am receiving every miracle that God has in His hands for me. As I am speaking, God is pouring forth miracles from his hands. Even now as I am speaking, God has commanded His angels concerning me to work on my behalf the supernatural experiences that I long to have. Today, I shall see miracles right before my eyes. I am receiving all the miracles that God has in store for me. God is doing for me the same miracles that I read about in the Holy Bible. I believe in the report of God, and I believe He loves me just as much as those He performed miracles for in the bible. Thank you great God for performing the supernatural in my every day life!

In Jesus' name, it is done.

26. Affirmation of Stillness

Be still and know that I am God (Psalms 46:10).

Stillness is something that each person wishing to inherit the promises of God, must practice. Have you ever sought God for guidance, instruction, and answers? I know I have. There have been many times I have sought God through prayer about things and have received guidance and answers to my prayers. I have discovered through several experiences that it is possible to receive answers to things we are concerned about through prayer. However, I have learned, through experience, that it is also very difficult to be still enough to allow the things that are revealed unto us through prayer happen. I learned to pray about everything. I felt like I had to discuss everything with the Lord. After some time, God began to show me things. I really felt special to be hearing from the Lord. It was beautiful to see things in my dreams and awake to have them happen.

At first, I thought it was strange, but the spiritual part of me was overjoyed that I had a special gift. After having things revealed to me while I lay asleep at night, I soon discovered that this was God's way of communicating with me.

I recall the first dream about eight years ago. I was in a relationship with Jasmine's father, and one night, I dreamt that he was planning a trip to Michigan without me. I remember waking up and telling him about the dream, and he just looked at me with a blank look on his face. When I returned home from work that evening, I discovered the dream was real. He actually purchased a plane ticket and was on his way to Detroit. I was furious because the rent was due and he did not pay it, but instead bought a ticket to go cheat and God only knows what else. This is one among several experiences I have had in my sleep.

I also recall having a dream that was a warning for my aunt. I dreamt we were walking in front of a hospital, and I was explaining to her that a young gentleman, by the name David, was sick with AIDS. I told her this several times, as we walked. When I awoke the next day, I called her and warned her to be careful, and if she met someone named David to be aware that he had AIDS. That afternoon, I came home from church and happened to call her on her cell phone, hoping to meet up with her for dinner. It was then when a man walked up to her and said, "Hi, my name is David."

I heard him introduce himself, and I screamed, "Oh, my God, that's him!"

My aunt then said, "I will call you right back."

Later she called me and said when the man introduced himself as David she became startled. I knew that God allowed me to warn her of the danger. These experiences I have had were more like visions.

The voice of God will heal you, change your life, destroy strongholds, make you think, act, and speak differently, and for certain make you know the truth about yourself. I was in a dead end relationship with Nia's father. I felt like I had to make things work out since we had a daughter together. I was afraid to fail in another relationship again. Jasmine never met her father, and I was determined to have Nia's father in our lives, no matter what it cost me. I suffered dearly every day while I fought to make things work with Nia's father. It was actually mental and emotional abuse. I knew he did not love me, but I did not care. It was a very dysfunctional relationship.

After two years of abuse, things seemed to mellow out between us. I remember one night I was lying in my bed and I prayed and asked God if I was doing the right thing by staying with a man who was not in love with me. I remember telling God that if He would just come and tell me the truth about my situation, I would listen and do whatever He said. That night as I lay asleep I heard the voice of God with my spiritual ears. This is what I heard.

"Shane is in love with his first child's mother. This is who he really wants to be with, and they are going to get back together."

When I awoke the next morning, those words were stuck in my head. I finally knew the truth. I looked at him and to be honest I was still in denial. That day, he said I should meet him at his mother's house. While we were there eating, the woman actually came over and talked with him in the kitchen for a long time. I had not yet told him about my dream. God again reminded of the words I heard and warned me that this would be my last chance to break free. After she left, I explained to him everything that I believed God told me in my dream. I was afraid to ask him if it was true because I did not want to lose him. Somehow, I found the courage to ask him if the words spoken to me in my sleep were true. I looked at him in his eyes hoping he would tell me the truth. He then stared into my eyes and said everything was true.

Tears welled up in my eyes and began to fall endlessly and I said, "Goodbye Shane."

Just a few months later, they moved in with one another and began to heal their past relationship. What God spoke to me was indeed true.

In the past I could never find the strength to stay away, however, this time was different. The words of God delivered me. I never desired to be with him again. Instantly, God took all those feelings away. Why? Because He spoke truth into my soul. From that day on, my life changed. I started college, and my whole life turned for the better. I then became infused with the knowledge of just how precious I was in the eyes of God. I stopped sleeping with men who cared absolutely nothing about me. I vowed to learn to love myself. I vowed to allow God to heal my wounds of the past. It has taken a lot of effort, and God is still working with me today. Once He spoke truth into my spirit, deliverance fell upon me. I was delivered from self-destructive behavior. I learned to love God, life, and myself.

All of the revelations and truths were revealed to me while I slept. It is in stillness we can hear instructions coming directly from the mouth of God. God spoke to many of our heroes from the bible while they were in a form of stillness. In other words, they were asleep. When you lie still and are at rest, God can speak to you. God has rarely spoken specific instructions to me while I was walking down the street or watching television.

Now there have been several occasions when God would lead me to an individual soul while I was out, and He would impress in my spirit what their issue was. He would lead me to pray for that individual concerning their need. For example, one Sunday morning, the girls and I were on our way to church. I stopped at a gas station to get some juice. While I was waiting in line, I sensed the woman standing in front of me was in some form of distress. My spirit led me to invite her to our church. When I asked her if she would like to come, her face immediately grew sad. The Holy Spirit then impressed these words in my spirit.

"She has lost someone real close to her. Pray with her."

I did not reveal to her what was revealed to me, but I did ask her if I could pray with her. We agreed to meet each other outside at her car. When I got there, she was flooded in tears; she explained to me that she had lost her father and that Sundays were always hard for her. We prayed together, and she then went on her way to work. This type of leading is somewhat different from the actual voice of God.

When one actually hears a word spoken from the Lord, that individual's life has no other alternative but to change. It is impossible to hear the voice of God and remain the same. I can only imagine exactly how Joseph felt when he discovered that the woman he was pledged to marry was with child. He probably felt embarrassed and shamed of his bride to be. He probably thought in his mind that Mary was a two-timer. I can just imagine her pleading with Joseph telling him, "Baby, the Lord did it!"

He probably thought she was nuts. I know he knew that the messiah was to come, but was He really coming through his bride to be? I am quite sure that Joseph sought the Lord for counsel regarding this situation. While Joseph lie asleep in the middle of the night an angel of the Lord appeared to him in a dream and spoke the word of truth in his spirit. The angel assured Joseph that it was okay for him to marry his bride to be and told him with whom she was pregnant. When Joseph awoke, he was no longer confused. He knew the truth, and he made Mary his bride. The key point I want to emphasize is that Joseph heard from God while he was in a form of stillness. He was asleep. He was resting. Had God not sent His messenger to speak to him, he may not have married the woman who was to birth the savior of this world.

An angel of the Lord revealed the revelations of Jesus Christ to the servant John, who wrote the book of revelations. In stillness, God can speak. In stillness, God can work things together for your own good. In stillness, God can change people's hearts and minds. In stillness, you can have rest and peace. In stillness, you can gain confidence in God by seeing Him at work in you, through you, and all around you. In stillness, those difficult situations that you face can be instantly turned around. There are answers in stillness. Being still and letting God be God in my life has been one of the most difficult challenges I had to learn to master. I just could not let God be God. I believed that God needed me to help Him work things out in my life. I did not understand that the only thing God needed me to be is STILL! I had not the slightest idea that all God required from me is to believe that nothing was impossible for Him to bring to pass in my life. That was all. Quite simple instructions I would say. I just could not do it.

I would pray about things and receive answers, but I just could not be still enough to let God bring me my heart's desires. I had to go snooping around in God's business. I had to help Him make the answers to my prayers happen. I just could not shut up, be still, and let things happen. I remember driving myself almost over the edge because I wanted the things that I believed God showed me to happen. I wanted them immediately. I became so anxious for the things God promised me that I did silly things at times. I now know better.

One day the Holy Spirit revealed to me these words, *"You have not yet learned to wait on me."*

When I heard this, I knew I was lacking the patience that is required in order for one to be still. I remember many days getting mad at God because I thought He was punishing me for some reason. I would tell myself that God has forgot all about Melissa. I would convince myself that He was mad at me. I would cry out to him day and night for help, but I still had not learned to wait on Him. I mean I tried to wait for Him, but the Lord was just taking too long. So there I went, running around trying to do things that only God could do. I finally learned after many lessons that when I became silent and still, God was at work in my life and my circumstances.

Speak these words of stillness into your life today!

I will be still and know that God is God. I will be still and know that God is in charge. I will be still and know that I am not in control. I will be still and know that God is. I will be still and know that God does. I will be still and know that God can do what I cannot do. I will be still and know that in my stillness I gain victory! In Jesus' name, it is done.

27. Affirmation To Defeat Self-Destructive Behavior

The way of the Lord is strength to the upright: but destruction shall be to the workers of iniquity (Proverbs 10:29).

Self-destructive behavior is any negative action that will inhibit you from fulfilling your purpose here on earth. It is also any action that eventually destroys you physically, mentally, and spiritually.

It was not until I was actually set free from self-destructive behaviors that I was able to look back on the behaviors of my past and have an understanding to what made me want to self destruct. I discovered the abuse I suffered throughout my childhood destroyed my self-esteem. I remember growing into my adolescent years believing that no one loved me. I thought that if my own mother did not love me enough to see to it that I grew into a healthy adult, then no one else would love me either. I remember feeling totally helpless and worthless throughout my childhood. I would often cry and wonder what could a little girl have done so wrong that her mother would walk away and never return. I was angry with everyone, including myself. For a while, I believed that it was my fault she ran away.

Being sexually molested as a child naturally raised my curiosity about sex. I did not know what it meant to be loved by someone. I had no idea that sex was designed for people who were united in marriage. When I became a young woman, I noticed that men were very much attracted to me. They would flirt with me and I enjoyed it.

Finally, someone was paying attention to me. It actually thrilled me. My first sexual experience that I willfully allowed occurred when I was thirteen years old. I thought that having sex would somehow link me to love. I thought that sex would make me feel accepted. I was so deceived.

As the years passed by, my body was used by men that were not in love with me. I was twenty-five years old when I realized that sex had nothing to do with an individual loving me. I realized that real love began on a spiritual level, with me growing intimate with God. Developing a relationship with God allowed me to understand that His love was real, and His love existed within my soul. I finally discovered that I could not possibly be in love with any man I ever had a relationship with because my soul felt broken. My soul felt wounded. My soul felt abandoned. My soul felt nothing but pain. My soul felt lost. Because my soul felt shattered into tiny little pieces, I could not ever begin to love healthy. I could never be loved in a healthy way, (the way every woman desires to be loved by someone), until the shattered pieces of my soul were put back together again.

But how could so many broken pieces be put back together? The concept of Melissa had been distorted. Who would help me? I knew for sure that I could not do it alone. I thought of going into therapy, however at the time I was afraid. I was afraid if I shared my experiences with a therapist, he or she would pass judgment on me and would not understand all the hell I have been through. I also remember thinking that no one would understand me anyway. I will say that therapy probably would have done me some good, however I know now that God had another pathway planned out ahead of me so that I could heal. I am sure if it were in His plan at that particular time, I would have seen a therapist. To this day, I am so grateful God chose to work with me himself. There is no greater therapist than the one who created me. God desired to reveal himself to me personally. God desired me to heal on a level that one day I would be able to help others heal.

My addiction to men, who were destructive to my soul, was the very first self-destructive behavior God revealed to me. God knew of

147

my childhood, and God knew why I was being promiscuous. He knew everything about me. That part of my soul that had been wounded sexually as a child longed to understand the true purpose of sexual intercourse. My soul longed for love and attention. God showed me that each time I lay down with a man and allowed him to enter me was a sexual sin. He showed me that sex itself was not the sin and that I was not sinning against Him, only against myself. My body was precious to Him and sacred to Him because He dwelled within me. God showed me that He loved me no matter what and nothing I ever did could separate me from his love, but I was hurting Melissa. God told me that I had to stop. God revealed to me that He grieved for me because He had a special plan for my life, and lying down with different men was not part of His plan, yet was a scheme of the enemy to destroy me. I understood exactly what God was showing me.

When I realized I was feeding an addiction, saddening God, and the devil was encouraging me to destroy myself, I knew I had to stop. I turned to the Lord for help. I no longer wanted to have sex with men so that I could feel loved. Just because I realized all of this does not mean that I stopped instantly. I should have, but I could not. The process was very difficult.

There were times when I would become involved with men and desired to have sex. I had to remember to think clearly and think of God's love for me and the love I had for myself. Most of all I had to remind myself that I was a new creature in Christ and Jesus saved me from death and destruction. I would feel an awful feeling in my stomach and was reminded that the individual person I was with was not in love with me nor was I in love with him. We were not in love with each other; we did not intend to spend the rest of our lives together; and we did not know each other well enough to actually connect our souls with one another. When I did end up sleeping with someone, afterwards I would lie there and tears would flow from my eyes because I knew I was wrong. I kept on fighting my addiction, and one day, I realized I was overcoming it.

It was during these experiences when I realized that the seed of love was developing inside of me and I now knew better. When I realized I loved God and myself too much to keep on letting men use me, I would then jump up and shout aloud, "I cannot do this! I love myself and I love God. God has a plan for my life and this is not part of the plan!"

After some years had passed, I knew I was getting better. I had healed from my addiction to sex in exchange for love.

If you struggle with sexual addictions, let me encourage you to overcome this stronghold on your life. If you are a woman, please understand that no matter how many men you sleep with, God will always love you. Also understand that no matter how many men you sleep with, true love will never be found in sharing your body with different men hoping and praying that this will be the one to love you. Please recognize that you are feeding an addiction. The love you are searching for is somewhere within you. God is the love you are searching for because God lives in you. God is waiting for you to realize that in Him is all the love you will ever need. Look to God and not man for love.

The enemy knows that if you keep on sleeping with different men in search for love, eventually, the plan that God has for your life will be hindered in some way. Unwanted pregnancies resulting in single parent households, the affliction of the disease AIDS, and wounds resulting in bitterness and sadness resulting from unproductive ungodly relationships. Take some time to get to know God. Allow Him to reveal himself to you, because when He begins to reveal himself to you, the seed of love awakens inside of you, and you will begin to realize you are worth more than thirty minutes (if that) of sex.

I understand the need and the desire to feel love from another human being, however you can never get someone to love you by having sex with them. The only thing you will get them to do is use you again. They may love the way you make them feel, and you may love the way they make you feel but always remember that God is love and since God lives within you, you are love. When you engage in sexual behavior with someone other than who you have chosen to spend the rest of your life with, and you have sex, mistakenly thinking that in exchange the other person will love you, you are engaging in self-destructive behavior.

Another form of self-destructive behavior I would like to share with you is probably one of the hardest addictions of which I had to be healed. I began smoking cigarettes for fun at the age of sixteen. I thought it was cute. I even believed it made me look sexy. My friend and I would steal her mother's cigarettes, go out in the back yard, and smoke them one by one. At first, they relaxed me when I felt tension. I felt cool. I can remember my friend and I looking at each other smiling as we puffed away.

I was twenty-one years old and expecting my first child when I realized that I could not quit. I had to do something, if not for me then for my unborn child. I stopped smoking in my seventh month of pregnancy. I had limited myself to two cigarettes per day before that. I praise God that my baby was born healthy. Shortly after Jasmine was born, I started back again. When I found I was expecting my second baby I stopped again when I was about five months. I could not quit for myself. After Nia was born I started smoking again, but this time I really desired to quit. I wanted to quit for me this time. I wanted to quit because I was finally beginning to love Melissa. I struggled to quit for my unborn babies, but as soon as they were born, I would start right back up again. I would pour all of my cigarettes into the toilet and flush them. I would then have such a craving that I would go right back out and buy another pack. I would smoke only one cigarette per day sometimes. I could hardly breathe. I would get bronchial infections all the time and I felt sick. I smelled like an ashtray.

I now look back and wonder how in the world did I ever convince myself that smoking was cute and sexy. How could I actually inhale into my lungs all those toxins? My lungs were made to exchange carbon dioxide for oxygen. And there I was, inhaling poison into my lungs. The frightening discovery was that subconsciously, I was doing this to myself on purpose. I knew cigarettes caused cancer. I remember one of my uncles passed away from lung cancer. Why?

Why could I not quit? I remember one day it was all so clear. I was praying, and I asked the Lord to help me quit smoking because nothing I did to try to stop seemed to help. I remember this still voice from within said, *You must understand why you smoke before you can quit.*

When I heard those words, I began to try to figure out why was I trying to kill myself. Each time I smoked, those words came back to me, and while I was puffing away, I would think,"Why am I doing this to myself. What is making me do this?"

One day, while I was smoking a cigarette, I figured it all out. I hated myself. I secretly wanted to self-destruct. I felt so unworthy about whom I was, and I subconsciously wanted to die. When I figured this all out, I was ready to heal myself of the self-destructive behavior that was making me smoke. I was ashamed that I was trying to kill myself and destroy the delicate pink lungs that God so skillfully created. Something needed to happen. I knew I could not do it all alone so I once again went to God for help.

While I was praying, I asked God again to show me why I kept on smoking. God revealed these words. *You have the desire to smoke within your heart. You have an addiction in your mind. You have a taste for cigarettes inside of your mouth. You have a craving within your lungs. You must be set free.*

The next day, I decided that I had to give smoking up, for myself and for God. A piece of God lived inside of me. How could He stand all of that filthy cigarette smoke? I wanted to live to see my grandchildren one day. I did not want to suffer a death of lung cancer. I wanted to love myself, not hate myself. I wanted to be set free.

The next day I wrote a prayer in the words that God spoke to my spirit that said: *God please take the addiction from my mind, please take the craving from my lungs, please take the taste from my mouth, and please take the desire for cigarettes from within my heart.* I also bought some chewing gum and chewed my jaws sore while redundantly reciting my prayer. I had not smoked in about seven days when I felt the desire to do away with the gum. I did not want to be addicted to chewing gum. All I had left was my prayer. I must have said that prayer at least thirty times a day for several months. Every time I would have an urge to smoke, I would affirm my special prayer. I have not smoked in five years. I have not desired to do so either. Once again, it was through prayer God delivered me from another self-destructive pattern.

I have learned through this experience that when we understand why we are doing some of the things we are doing, it is then when we can begin to heal from self-destructing patterns. I am thankful for that voice within my soul who revealed information to me that would save my life. That voice is the awesome voice of God. That voice did not say many words, but the few it spoke to me delivered me from the self-destructive spirit of smoking.

About two years ago, I met a young woman who worked at the college I attended. She invited me to her house, and at the time, she was going through many problems. She too smoked cigarettes. She was telling me that she wanted to be set free from everything. I began to pray that same prayer for her. I shared with her how God had delivered me from that stronghold of smoking. I gently explained to her everything God explained to me. I also told her the truth. I explained to her that somewhere within her subconscious, she hated herself and she wanted to die. I explained to her that I was healed from accepting this as the truth. We prayed and thanked God for her deliverance. The next day, I called her to see how she was doing. She said she was very ill and was vomiting. I knew she was under God's power of deliverance, but I said nothing. Some weeks later she said, "Melissa, I do not know what you did, but every since you said that prayer with me, I have not touched a cigarette." She also said that she ended an abusive relationship with the man she had been living with.

Two years passed by and the woman has been set free. I know I was not the one who set her free from smoking. Those words God spoke to me were what set her free. There is power and deliverance in the words of God. I want to tell you that smoking is very addictive and a very difficult habit to break, but if you pray and ask God for insight, I am sure He will help you. It is not His will for any of us to perish, and if we seek help, He is always there to assist us. Let me encourage you to begin to pray this prayer if you are one who desires to quit smoking. I know if God did it for my friend and I, I know He will do it for you.

Pray this anointed prayer each day as many times as you need to.

Father God, I ask that you wipe the taste I have for cigarettes from my mouth. I ask that you remove the craving from my lungs. I ask that you take the addiction from my mind, but most of all I ask that you remove the desire that I have to smoke from within my heart. I thank you that you are doing this now even as I am speaking. In Jesus' name, Amen.

Self-destructive behavior is actually the enemy's way of hindering you from fulfilling God's ultimate plan for your life. Satan knows that if he can cut your life short, whether it is by cancer, AIDS, suicide, alcoholism, or drugs use, then you cannot be used to make this world a better place. You cannot fulfill your purpose operating under these dark influences. We all must die one day, but why make choices that will speed along the process. Satan also knows that you were put here to make this world a better place through your loving thoughts and actions towards others. He also knows that hell is his destiny, and he wants to take as many souls with him as possible. Did you know God grieves when a precious life is wasted, meaning a life lived without a purpose?

You are engaging in self-destructive behavior if you are doing anything that brings harm to yourself. You are engaging in self-destructive behavior if you are doing anything that does not bring you happiness, joy, or success. I encourage you today to look over your habits and judge whether they are self-destructive habits. If you are self-destructing, I encourage you to begin to call on the name of Jesus for help. It was in the name of Jesus I was set free from many self-destructive behaviors, and I know it will be in the name of Jesus that you too will be set free.

Father,

I ask in Jesus' name that you send your burden removing power upon the one reading this book. I ask that you bind up any stronghold that this person may be dealing with. God I know there is power in the name of Jesus. I ask the same power that set me free from self-destruction be released upon this person. I thank you that you have heard this prayer for I always knew that you hear me when I pray. In Jesus name, it is done.

Speak these affirming words into your life today:

I no longer wish to self-destruct. I will no longer self-destruct. I will not engage in any more self-destructive behavior. I will not destroy the precious gift of life that has been granted to me. I love myself and will not hate myself another day by subconsciously self-destructing. From this day on, I will strive towards excellence and figure out why God has me here and what would He have me do. Instead of self-destructing, I am now reconstructing my mind, my body, and my spirit. Thank you God for freedom from self-destruction. In Jesus' name, it is done.

28. Affirmation: To Walk in a Life of Ministry

Whereof I was made a minister, according to the gift of the grace of God given unto me by the effectual working of his power (Ephesians 3:7).

If you are anything like me, at some point in your life, you have probably desired to invest time into your community or at your local church. I was really pressed for time and could not seem to be involved much at church. When I did try to become involved in different things it seemed as if I was not allowed to participate. I desired to begin a single parents' ministry, but the door seemed as if it was shut in my face. I felt as though because I was an unwed mother, I was looked down upon by others in my church. I felt as if the church did not support single mothers and that is why the ministry could not be birthed. I did not become angry because I could not begin the ministry. I trusted that my leader knew what was best at the time. I trusted that he saw things more clearly than I and he probably saw that I was not ready to handle the task of a single parents' ministry. My feelings were hurt and I did feel disappointed, yet I still loved and supported my leaders decision. After this incident, I felt pushed away from the church. I gave up trying to become involved in my church and I decided to become involved with in my community. I realized that God had His reasons for things happening and I decided I was going to help people no matter what other people thought or said about me. I made myself a minister in the eyes of the

Lord.

I decided to make my every day life a ministry. I realized that there was much more ministry out in my community then there was in the church. I wanted each day to be lived with honest intentions and purpose. I decided that my job would be my place of ministry. I worked at a hospital. I finally realized that the hospital was the place where God was going to use me. I realized that I was on a special assignment from God. My job was pretty laid back. I was to deliver drugs to the computer system at certain times throughout the day. I worked on weekends, and the shifts were between twelve and sixteen hours. I began to spend a lot of time praying in the chapel at the hospital. Sometimes I would go sing and pray to the Lord.

Trying to keep up with my grades at school, my children, my home, and work to pay the bills was pretty difficult. I would try to finish all my deliveries early so that I could have time to study. Studying at work on my breaks saved me precious time that I spent with the girls at home. I did my best to balance it all out, but I would always fall short. Sometimes, I would stay up all night studying after I settled the girls into bed. No matter how hard I tried to keep up with everything, I would find myself pouring my soul out to God and saturating the altar in the chapel with tears.

I found my help and strength through having long heart felt conversations with God right there in the chapel. I would tell God how hard my life was and that I needed Him to help me make it. I prayed constantly for God's power and blessing to help me make it through. When I would finish praying and crying out to God, it seemed as if the pressure was released from my soul. I would also pray and ask God to let me cross someone's path who may need to know Jesus. No matter how busy I was, I felt led to reach out and help the patients at the hospital. Soon, the Lord began to send the lost and helpless my way. I was so excited to be working for the Lord. I would pray with people, laugh with people, and feed those who were hungry. I considered myself a minister. No, I was not an actual minister recognized in church, but I believed I was a minister in eyes of God. I became less involved in my church, but God was using me to lead others to His house, restore hope to their souls, and to introduce them to Jesus Christ.

The most wonderful act of ministry that ever took place at the hospital was one that deeply moved my spirit. I vowed to myself that I was not going up to the thirteenth floor (the psychiatric ward) at the hospital for a long time after one of the patients flashed me. Now that I think back, it is somewhat funny, but believe you me, when it happened it was very upsetting. I turned around and there was a heavy-set man who had written all over his clothes with red ink coming towards me. He stopped and pulled down his pants and showed me everything he had. I screamed, "What are you doing, mister?"

He murmured a few words that I could not understand and began towards me again. This time I yelled, "You better back up buddy or I am going to kick you where it hurts!"

The security guard escorted him out and said he was harmless.

The next day I had to deliver some drugs to that floor, and I hesitated. I was going to ask someone to make the delivery for me, but the spirit of God impressed me to take it myself. I was getting ready to get off the elevator when a man in distress called out to me, "Please help me, I am addicted to crack cocaine and I need help!"

At first, I did not know what to say. I froze in silence. My heart was pounding. This poor man was crying out to me for help. I did not know what to do at first, but then, the Holy Spirit clearly spoke into my spirit that I was to help him be delivered. I told him he would need deliverance. I asked him did he want to be delivered. He sighed. "Yes, please help me."

We rode the elevator down to the chapel. I took him to the altar and asked him to get on his knees and begin to thank the Lord for his deliverance in the name of Jesus. He did so, and I began to pray over him and call on the name Jesus. I felt the presence of God over us. The power of God was with us. The man began to cry out to the Lord begging for forgiveness. My eyes flared with tears of joy as I prayed and praised God. I began to sing songs of praise as he was calling out to God. He began to ask for forgiveness for his sins and all the hurt and pain he caused his mother and family members due to his drug addiction.

I remember him crying these words. "Lord, I am so sorry I hurt my momma. I promise you Lord I won't ever steal from her again."

He kept crying this repeatedly. He said many other things, but I remember what he said about his mom most of all. My heart filled with gladness and compassion for him. We stayed in the chapel singing and praying for about an hour. He received Jesus as his personal savior that day and was set free. He thanked me and told me he was checking into the rehab program provided at the hospital so he would not be on the streets any longer.

My heart was touched by the man's deliverance. I was so happy that God was using me to help set another soul free and lead them to Jesus Christ. I fully understand that the power of God set Him free, and God used me as a vessel to lead him to the altar for the process to begin.

There were also times God used me to pray with families who had sick family members in the hospital. Since Grady Hospital serves the poor, there are many hungry people always asking for food. All that I could think about was, *He who lends to the poor, lends to the Lord, but he who shuts his ears to the cries of the poor shall too cry out to God and not be heard.*

I felt responsible to feed someone if that person asked me. I knew each person who asked was starving, because that person would not ask for money, but for a burger from McDonald's. I began to feel like God placed all these people in my pathway because He knew He could count on me to do what was necessary to assist them. So you see even though I was a pharmacy employee, God was using me as a minister. I share these experiences not to boast on what I do for others, but to simply say that whatever you do, you can be a minister. You can make your life into a ministry simply by asking God to send others who need help, your way.

If you are one that feels like you want to do something to make your life more meaningful, I challenge you today to begin to live meaningful. Do meaningful things, speak meaningful things, and think meaningful things. Begin to make your life a ministry. Visit the elderly people in convalescent homes. If someone tells you he or she is hungry, do not say no, feed the person. There are so many people who are caught up in thinking that ministry can only be done in the church. This is so far from the truth. You can have your own ministry by walking your every day life as a minister. I believe when God sees that we are walking in a life of ministry every day and in everything we do, He will then bring others our way, and open doors for ministry for us.

The little things count the most to God. The little things you do mean a lot to the one your helping and are great things in eyes of God. Therefore, you do not have to get mad because they will not let you exercise your gifts in church, just exercise them in your every day life and watch God begin to enlarge your territories. If you can sing and feel like you cannot be heard in church for some reason, then go sing for the elderly in nursing homes; they would be so thrilled. Many of them are very lonely and would enjoy your company.

If you feel like you have been called to preach the word of God, go speak to the young men and women that are on the streets selling drugs and their bodies. Prepare a sermon just for them. You see, it's very rare that a drug dealer or prostitute come to church, however if you go to their neighborhood, you'll see a group of them just hanging out. Go and minister to that group of drug dealers and encourage them to get off the streets.

Do you get the point I am trying to make? I am not saying that you should not preach in church , but I can guarantee that if you are faithful in what you think is least, God will make you a ruler of many things. Everything you do can be a ministry if that is what you desire it to be. Let everything that you do be done as unto the Lord. Do not be discouraged if you feel like there is nothing for you to do in church. Do not get angry with your leader and leave church just because you can not do what you feel you are to do in church. Trust God, wait for God, and begin to serve in your community. Think things over and make ministry happen in your everyday life. Today, ordain yourself as a minister in the eyes of God. Begin today to live a life of ministry everywhere that you go.

Speak a life of ministry into your surroundings today!

I am a minister of God. My life is a ministry for God. My home is a ministry for God. My marriage is a ministry for God. My job is a ministry for God. My everyday walk is a ministry for God. From this day on, I will live my life in a meaningful way and with a meaningful purpose. And that purpose is a life called to minister to those in need. Thank you great God for calling me to walk in an everyday life of ministry. For today, I am an ordained minister. In Jesus' name, it is done!

29. Affirmation to Maintain Healthy Relationships

And the Lord God said: "It is not good for man to be alone; I will make a suitable partner for him. And the Lord caused a deep sleep to fall upon Adam, and he slept: and He took one of his ribs and closed up the flesh instead thereof: and the rib which the Lord God had taken from man, made he a woman, and brought her unto the man. Therefore shall a man leave his father and his mother, and shall cleave unto his wife; and they shall be one flesh"(Genesis2: 18, 21-22, 24).

Everyone desires a healthy, loving relationship. God intended for us to fellowship with one another. He desires for a man and a woman to become one by the union of a marriage. He desires human beings to live in peace and harmony with each other.

Over the years, I often wondered if a man and a woman had to be married in order to lay with each other like husband and wife? The bible teaches us against the sinful act of fornication. When I decided to become intimate with God and walk continuously in obedience to all that He commands me to do, I knew that I had to quit committing acts of fornication. I often wondered why God would prohibit me from doing something that I enjoyed doing, especially something that felt so wonderful. What if I never got married? Would that mean that I could never have intimacy with a man again? Thinking those thoughts was quite disturbing to me.

I loved God, but I also wanted to be in a productive relationship with a man that I could make love to. I, like any other normal human being, desired to be married. I did not like the idea that I had to choose between man and God. I figured that if God made me, then He also knew that I had needs and desires. Why should I have to choose? As you can see, I was confused. The church taught me that I had to be pure and holy. I was trying my best to quit fornicating. I already had two children, and I did not want to end up with three. I fought the temptations of fornication. I promised myself I would not have sex anymore unless I got married. I decided to wait as long as it took for the right man to come into my life.

I listened to religious tapes and attended single conferences to keep my mind focused on God. I remember listening to one religious tape that said I would need to prepare to be a wife. The speaker on the tape told me that I had to keep my house clean, keep plenty of soap powder, and learn how to budget my money. I understood this part, and I already was doing these things, yet I still was not married. I agreed with everything she was saying, but then she said that I should not desire to be married if I was poor and did not own my own home. I thought to myself, *Well, I guess I can hang up the desire to married because I do not have a lot of money and it will be a long time before I finish school.* I remember feeling sad after listening to the tape. I could not understand why I could not be married due to my circumstances. After listening to the tape, I examined myself and I concluded from the speakers words, that because I did not have a lot of money and because I did not own my own home, I did not deserve to be married.

Did it not matter that my heart was good and that I was full of so much love? Did it not matter that I wholeheartedly loved God, and I always put Him first in my life? I thought that working towards my goals and dreams and putting God first should give an account for something. I thought as Christians, we should see things through the eyes of the spirit as God does. I thought we should look at the heart of someone whom we chose to spend the rest of our lives with instead of looking at how much money he had or what kind of car he drove. I felt like I was attractive on the outside, but I made a special effort to gleam with beauty from the depths of my soul. For God's sake, I was trying to get it together! I was also taught that the Lord was working on me. I heard this over and over again. I liked the idea that God was actually taking His time to prepare me, but I heard that I was being worked on so much, after a while I began to feel like something was terribly wrong with me. I began to wonder just how long will the Lord be working on me. I began to turn away from people since I was being worked on and I figured something must be wrong with me. With time, God balanced my mind. I now know that God was really preparing me for the life long commitment of marriage and this time of preparation really did take a lot of work. I knew that the teaching was right, but I just hated to have someone tell me I had to be worked on. It made me sick, but yet I waited and let God work on me. I felt as though no one would ever be perfect and God would actually be working on me until the day I die. I just could not understand why I was not ready. I thought I was ready, but God did not.

I also remember the church teaching me that I should not be with a man who did not have the means to provide for me. After all, the husband is the head of the household and he needs to be able to provide everything that I need. I accepted this as the truth. I actually liked the idea that the man who was to be my husband, should be able to take of me. As I matured in my spirituality, I came to the conclusion that yes, I had more maturing to do before I entered the ministry of marriage, yes, the man is to be the provider, and no, I should not marry someone who did not have the skills to be a provider. However, I also concluded that how much money he made or the kind of car that he drove had nothing to do with his ability to be a good provider or a good husband. I also understood that a marriage does require financial responsibility.

I did some research and found that a large percentage of marriages end in divorce because of financial burden. I knew that it would be important for me to become financially stable so that I would be able to contribute something to my marriage. I also accepted that just because I did not have a lot of money, it did not mean that I did not deserve to be married. I made up in my mind I was worthy of being loved regardless of my financial situation or how many material things that I possessed simply because I am a representation of God, simply because He lives inside of me, and simply because He created me to be a help to the right man at the right time. I decided that I would not let some lady on a religious tape fill my head with the idea that I should not be thinking about marriage unless I had a lot of money and my own home.

Every day, I thought of marriage. I thanked God that when He thought I was ready to handle the ministry of marriage I would marry. Another truth I accepted from church teachings was the man is the leader, and I was going to have to submit to him. I accepted the teachings that my husband would be in leadership over my two daughters and me. I remember asking God to please send who He would have to be in my life because I could not submit to a fool. I also made up in my mind that I would not judge a man because he did not have a lot of money. I decided to pray and ask God for guidance and answers concerning each man that presented himself to me. I decided if God did not approve, then neither would I. When I dated, I watched and prayed continuously for behaviors that I knew would be trouble in the future such as possessiveness and jealously.

I decided that if he loved God, demonstrated providing skills and stability, understood his godly role as a husband, was responsible, could love and accept my girls as his own, and loved me unconditionally in spite of my flaws and imperfections, then he could possibly be husband material. I learned from many hard lessons to discern the spirit of a man by the fruits that he bares.

People marry for all the wrong reasons. The divorce rate for Christians is just as high as people who are not Christians. Why? I believe it is because of religious tapes like the one I heard. It is because of false teachings about love and marriage. I have observed that people can own a home, have a lot of money, and have everything together, but can still end up spending the rest of their lives alone. I knew people who seemed like they had it all together. So why were they still alone? They were still alone because of the false teachings with which they have allowed others to poison their minds. Material things, rather than things of the Spirit, consumed them. Their truth about love has been distorted. They believed they could not marry anyone who had less than they had. What a big deception. They would actually refuse to date anyone who did not drive a certain kind of car. They would use the word of God to make excuses for their selfish behaviors. They would say,"The bible says do not be unequally yoked."

I used to think that too, but with spiritual maturity, I learned the truth. The bible says this to warn believers to be equally yoked in the spirit with others. This scripture has nothing to do with money and material things. We must be equally yoked with our mate in the spirit. I would listen to them tell me, "When you get to where you want to be in life and start making a lot of money, you will then understand what we mean."

I understood that successful people desire other successful people. I knew where they were coming from, but it disappointed me that when these successful individuals married other successful individuals only to be divorced a couple of years later. Why? Because they married based upon the accomplishments of each other's material success instead of their spiritual accomplishments and success. It really disappointed me to find that these successful people were having adulterous affairs outside of their marriage years later. When a man and a woman become married to each other based on material things, the marriage is set up for failure. Observing these tragic material-based marriages, I knew that when my time for marriage came, it would be a decision based on the riches of the spirit rather than the riches of this world.

I decided to go to the Lord myself for answers and to pray that at the right time to send me my spiritual partner and to reveal to me whom he would be. It was through prayer and patience that I gained wisdom concerning the ministry of marriage. When God said a man should leave his mother and father and cleave to his wife, He meant that the two should become one. An actual ceremony of marriage does not make a man and a woman become one. A ceremony is only symbolic unto men. When a man and a woman exchange marriage vows, they are affirming to God what they will do for each other throughout the marriage.

The man and woman become one when they join in sexual union with one another. Sexual intercourse joins their souls together as one. Sexual intercourse unifies a man and woman's soul, therefore they become one, taking on the personality of one another. Why would I want to become one with someone whom I was not going to spend the rest of my life with? I began to think that I was married and one in the spirit with each man I ever slept with. This was quite disturbing and frightening. I stopped fornicating and asked God to cleanse my soul.

God also revealed to me that I must first learn to maintain healthy relationships with the people who were already in my life before I could have a healthy marriage with a man. I could not get along with my aunt most of the time. She would say things to provoke me, and I would then say mean things to hurt her feelings. Would I do the same things in a marriage? Yes, and it would be quite damaging. Words can either edify a marriage or destroy it. At least when I get mad at my auntie, I can slam the phone down and stop talking to her for a couple of days. At least we live in separate houses.

If I behaved that way in my marriage, where would I go then? Words used inappropriately in a marriage are very damaging to the soul. God allowed me to realize that before I could function well in a marriage, I would have to learn to stop saying mean things when someone provoked me. I needed to learn to hold my tongue instead of saying whatever I felt I needed to say. It was very difficult to keep quiet when people were saying crazy things to provoke me, but I learned that some things shouldn't be said. I had a long way to go, but at least I was willing to do the work. We must learn to function well in all of our friendships and relationships with others in order to cope in a marriage.

Another important subject I would like to discuss is the idea that there is just one person for you. God does have someone designed for you, but because of all of the misconceptions about love, few people end up being with the mate that God designed for them. I discovered through experience that you might be compatible with several people.

I had so many questions for God. I began to wonder if I actually came from a man. The only man I knew who contributed to me being here was my father. What was God doing when He took a man's rib and made a woman? What did all of this mean? I began to receive answers to my questions. The reason I desired to be married was because my soul actually longed to reunite with my spiritual partner, whom I was once one within the spirit before I came here.

I realized that God did take woman from out of a man. In the flesh, both male and female are born through the womb of a woman. Yes we do bring forth life which is amazing and a wonderful mystery, yet we all come from the seed of a man. Men carry within their testicles the seed for a potential human life. The potential for a human life to become possible exists through a man. In order for life to be brought forth, the woman must grow, develop, nurture, and then bring forth life. Man and woman work together as one. One cannot do without the other.

Through the eyes of the spirit, I believe that God has taken each soul of a woman from the soul of a man. A soul is an immortal body that lives on forever. It is a form of energy that cannot be recreated neither can it be destroyed. It is who it is forever. God knew us in the spirit before we were even born. He knew His purpose for creating us. He also knew whom He would at the appropriate time, send in our lives. Because of the misconception of love, so many people have been deprived of experiencing a soul-to-soul connection with their ordained spiritual partner.

I believe if God knows the number of hairs on my head, then why would He not know with whom I was to spend the rest of my life? If He knows when you get up and when you lie down, why would He not know with whom you are to spend the rest of your life? The truth is, He does. I believe in the spiritual realm, there is one woman existing within a man. When God allowed your soul to come into the world to experience the gift of life, He also ordained your spiritual partner that right too. You and your spiritual partner were one before you were born and are destined to reunite on the physical plane at the appointed time. Even though God split your union and separated you from your spiritual partner, He did not intend for you to stay apart. He destined for you to meet again at the appointed time, here on earth.

When spiritual soul partners meet, they are very much alike and may feel as they have known each other for a lifetime. This is because they have. They were once joined by God in the spiritual realms and are being reunited in the physical to experience a life of intimacy together and fulfill a mission and purpose together on earth. They feel a sense of peace with each other and usually spend a lifetime together. When the two souls connect again, the search is over, the longing is satisfied, and the two spend the rest of their days on earth together.

It is good to know that God has always believed in the union of a man and a woman in the spiritual world and here in the physical world. This is why the human being longs to feel love. We always feel as though something is missing. That is why a man is always in search for his bride. This is why men hunt. It is not only a physical desire, but also a deep craving in his soul that has to be satisfied by reuniting with his long lost spiritual partner. I also believe that if two people marry and are together for all the wrong reasons, adulterous affairs begin. Why? Because the man is not one with whom he was one with in the spirit before being born. The desire for something else is always there. He still searches simply because he became one with the wrong soul. I also believe that when two spiritual partners reunite, the craving and searching subsides. I do not believe problems will never arise between them, but I do believe that they are far much easier to resolve than problems between two souls that are not connected.

Society believes that cheating is all a physical desire, which is true, however, the truth is that a man can never feel totally satisfied if his soul is always in want. He needs to find that part of himself that is missing. Just because a man marries a woman, does not mean that the deepest part of his soul is content and at peace. It does not mean that his soul has connected with who God intended to connect him with. A lot of men, especially Christian men, get trapped into unconnected marriages due to the biblical teaching "it is better to marry than to burn". They take this scripture and run in the wrong direction with it resulting in an dissatisfied marriage. His physical needs are met, yet after some time the desire to hunt resurfaces itself and he then begins to crave for that soul connection that God intended for him have. It is only a matter of time before his soul begins cry out again searching and yearning for a connection.

Even though married, his soul yet yearns for his true spiritual partner. As a result, adultery begins. Many men do not really understand their own spiritual selves or their feelings so they give different excuses for their acts of adultery. Some says it's an addiction. Some say it was a mistake. Some say they aren't physically attracted to their wife any more. These could very well be valid reasons, but few men are able to search deep within their souls and call it what it is- faulty decision making. It takes a man filled with the love of God within himself to honestly admit that he made a mistake in the person he has chosen as his life-partner. Today, there are few men who can say the words Adam affirmed, *"She (this) is now bone of my bones, and flesh of my flesh: she shall be called woman because she was taken out of me (man)."*

Adultery begins from an unsatisfied soul. It is not only the lusts of his flesh. When a man's soul is not content, he then looks for contentment elsewhere. When a man's soul is content, he is content and satisfied. A woman can do her very best to satisfy her husband physically but if she cannot quench the desires of his soul, there is really no hope. He will always be searching for that contentment he desires. This search usually results in adulterous affairs.

What do men and women do anyway? They marry for what they see with their natural eye and that is the outward appearance of a woman or a man. They discover later, after it is well too late, that their soul is unsatisfied. An unsatisfied soul is a partial answer to why men and women cheat.

It is so important to make a spiritual decision about marriage through constant prayer, because if we do not, then trouble, heartache, and pain lie ahead. Lack of spiritual insight, lack of patience, and misconceptions about love are the main reasons we become involved in unhealthy relationships and marriages. God knows what is best for each of us, and if we learn to make our decisions about marriage through the fruits of a person's spirit and prayer, I truly believe that spiritual partners would reunite, resulting in spiritual satisfaction and life-long marriages.

My grandparents were married over fifty years. Were they spiritual partners from the beginning? I'd like to believe so. Their marriage was not based upon money or how much the other person had. Their marriage was not established through each of their successes. They were a poor African American couple moving from the South, hoping to build a life and family together. Their marriage was united because they loved each other, and it lasted a lifetime. Although love cannot pay the bills, love will sustain a man and a woman through hard times. When money runs out there is always the bond of love. Love will make you stay in your marriage even if the two of you lose everything you have. Here are some words of wisdom from the Holy Spirit for those who desire to become married. *"The marriage built on material things and what the world calls success, is doomed for failure, but the marriage built on the foundation of the fruits of the spirit is one that lasts a lifetime."*

Sometimes spiritual partners manifest themselves as a few pounds over weight, a darker or lighter shade of skin, a different race all together, not rich, not proud and boastful, long hair, short hair, poor, who knows what else. What do we do? We pray for true love, but when it shows up, we cannot seem to accept it. I remember my favorite line, "I am not ready for this!"

I have told guys this many times. Now that I think back, if I was not ready, then why in the world was I praying every day for God to send me the love of my life?

Stop asking God to send someone into your life if you know you are not ready. Just ask God to place in your life who He has in mind for you when your mind, heart, and soul are ready to receive them. Pray for wisdom to discern whom the person may be. Ask God to prepare you for the ministry of marriage. When someone presents himself or herself to you, do not start nit picking and trying to find things wrong with them. Search the person's spirit. Make judgments based on the fruits that they are bearing. Get to know the person. Go ahead and give that person a chance to love you and give yourself a chance to experience true happiness. If you cannot do this, then I suggest that you keep this book very close to you and begin to affirm the affirmations written in the chapters, so that you can begin to have a change of heart, mind, and your words.

I have learned through experience that God will at least one time in your life present you with a spiritual partner fit just for you, yes, the one who you were with in the spirit world. However, when your spiritual partner shows up and you choose not to accept him or her, then it is your choice. God does not get upset with you, but who you do decide to spend the rest of your life with, whatever hard aches you may experience from your own choices is a result of your decision making and has nothing to do with God.

If you do pass your spiritual partner by, do not think that there will never be anyone else for you. You will meet someone else, and you can be happy. I just feel that when we choose whom God chooses, then blessings, real love, and happiness are in our best interests. If you are married, do not start wondering if you married the wrong person (you should know by now). Remember a marriage vow is for life and should never be broken. Learn to live with the choices that you have made, and make the best of the relationship that you have chosen to be in for life.

For those of you who are single, when you pray for a spiritual partner and God presents the person to you, put away all of your pride and arrogance. Remember with real love, there can be no pride. Make your decision based on the contents of the individual's heart. If a potential spiritual partner presents himself or herself to you, here are the things that you should ask yourself. Does this person love God? Does this person love himself or herself? Are the contents of this person's heart pure (remember you will know a tree by the fruits that he or she bears)? Does this person shine with inner beauty as well as his or her outward appearance? Does this person have dreams and goals in action? Is this person responsible? Does this person connect with my soul? The most important question that you can ever ask is, Father, is this the man or woman whom you have designed just for me?

If the answer is yes to these questions, then I would suggest that you give that person a chance. Do not be led by the false misconceptions being taught in today's time because you will end up disappointed. You may end up married to someone who has a lot of money, but has not a lot of love. You lose. You may end up with a tall dark handsome muscular man, but how many times is he going to cheat on you before he infects you with AIDS. Again, you lose (your life). You may end up with a beautiful woman who has all of the outward appearances that you desire, but she has no spiritual beauty. You lose. You may pass by a beautiful person who wholeheartedly loves life, God, and spirit. A person who loves you because he or she loves himself or herself, but because of pride and the lack of spiritual judgment, you end up missing out on a chance for true love.

If you are one who struggles with pride, I suggest you pray as I have and ask God to develop your spiritual insight, allowing you to see others for the essence of their soul instead of outward appearances. Remember you do not know whom God will present you with as your spiritual partner, but know that he or she is out there and you will come across that person eventually. Be prepared mentally, physically, and spiritually because it will happen and you do not want to miss an opportunity to spend the rest of your life with your spiritual partner.

Also remember, if you feel you missed this opportunity because of selfishness or pride, do not worry. You never know, if God has ordained a spiritual partner for you and has destined you two to be together to fulfill a purpose, maybe you will have another opportunity to be together when you are spiritually prepared.

Mend broken relationships with people, work through your issues, and try to consistently walk in the spirit of love. Your chance for love is coming, but you must learn to have healthy relationships with the people that are in your life now, you must learn to use spiritual judgment when making a decision to marry, and most of all you have to learn to pray when people present themselves to you. If you cannot get along with your friends and family, how will you get along with your husband or wife? God is watching everything that we do, and if we do not learn to work through relationships and resolve issues in a peaceful way, then there is a great possibility that we will not have successful productive marriages.

Speak these words to develop healthy relationships into your life today.

Today, I will make an effort to make my relationships with others healthier. Today, I am going to begin to resolve issues and problems in my present relationships. Today, I will begin to see others and determine their value based on the contents of their heart with my spiritual eyes as God does. Today, I will not evaluate people because of their present circumstances, but by the fruits of their spirit and their love for God. Today, I accept what God desires for me. Today, I will prepare myself spiritually, mentally, and physically for the day my spiritual partner and I meet. I will be ready when the time comes. Today, I am practicing love in all of my relationships. In Jesus' name, it is done.

30. The Ability to Dream

Then was the secret revealed unto Daniel in a night vision. Then Daniel blessed the God in heaven (Daniel 2:19).

As I was growing up, I can remember my grade-school teachers encouraging me to follow my dreams. I did not really understand what they were saying to me then, however now I understand what they meant. I have lived long enough now to understand that when I dream, I am being guided by the spirit of God towards healing and success. I have found that dreams are an avenue for us to heal and become that which we were created to be. I first learned of my ability to dream about eight years ago. Jasmine's dad and I were living together at the time and our relationship was rocky. I knew in my spirit that I was not planning to be with him much longer, but I needed time to develop a plan to prepare to leave.

One night as I lay asleep I dreamed that he bought a plane ticket and was going to Michigan. When I awoke, I said, "Baby, I dreamed you were going home."

He just stared at me with a blank look on his face and did not say anything, so I just brushed it off as just another dream. When I returned home from work, I found him all packed up and ready to head off to the airport without saying goodbye. I asked him where he was going, and he said he was taking a trip home to visit his daughter. I asked him why he planned a trip without me, and he said he needed time away. I then asked him why he did not tell me he was going when I told him I dreamed about it. He said he did not feel like fighting with me about visiting his daughter. He said he was going to leave a note for me on the kitchen table. I was very upset. I knew he was not only going to visit his daughter but he was going to visit her mother as well. I also knew that she was going to call me and tell me that they did everything under the sun, as was with the last trip he made.

I figured the least he could do was inform me ahead of time that he was leaving. We ended up having a very serious argument. While he was away, I decided it was time for me to leave. I thought of the dream I had and began to feel as though it was a warning to end the relationship. Therefore, I promised myself that if he ever planned another surprise trip without including me, it would be over. This was the first dream I recall having that actually happened.

When I began my journey towards a spiritual walk with God, I started dreaming regularly. I remember working with a young lady who had a drinking problem, which I knew nothing about until I dreamt that I was warning her if she kept on drinking it was going to kill her. I did not recall the dream until I saw her the next morning and she asked me to get one of the children a drink. I do not know what happened, but when she said drink, it reminded me of the whole dream and before you know it, I was telling her of the dream I had. She then explained to me that her mother died of liver failure due to alcohol. I did not think much of it until I told my best friend about the dream, whom I also worked with at the time. She asked me how I knew the girl had a drinking problem. I told her I did not. Then she told me all about it and that was serious. From this point on, I knew that I had a special gift.

I finally accepted that things were revealed to me in the form of dreams. I felt scared at first because I did not understand that it was a special gift to be able to see visions while I lay asleep at night. I also remember a time I was due for a promotion at my job, and I dreamed I was in the office with my boss and her administrator. In the dream, we were arguing about something. The next day, sure enough, we were all in the office and they were telling me that I was not going to get the promotion. My feelings were hurt because I knew I was doing the best job that I could do, and for them to deny me a promotion that was due to me was wrong. I gently explained to the two ladies that I was prepared for this conversation in a dream the night before, and I also explained that it did not matter to me if I was promoted or not because I was tired of black people always trying to hold each other back. I then left the office almost in tears. I prayed about it and two weeks later, they called me into the office again and informed me that I would receive the promotion I desired.

Dreams, whether they are visions of the future or are visions of our deepest desires, are crucial for the human soul. While we lay asleep at night, our bodies may be relaxed and at rest, but our spirits are always alert. While we lay asleep, our bodies are at work replenishing itself, making our spirits available to communicate with God. Many times, we are so preoccupied all day long that we could not communicate with God even if we tried. I like to believe God designed rest so that we may hear from him.

If you study the bible, you will discover that God communicated with His servants while they lay asleep at night. He spoke to them in their dreams and even sent heavenly beings to reveal certain information to them. God also carried his servants away in the spirit to show them divine revelations of heaven. As I studied the bible, I then felt more comfortable with my dreams. I was no longer afraid nor did I feel strange. I concluded that this was God's way of communicating with me. I actually felt very special that God would show me things as He did his servants of the bible.

My two babies and I lived in some low income housing in downtown Atlanta. It was a very frightening experience. The apartment itself was not bad. It had brand new carpet and fresh paint. It had two bedrooms. It was all I could afford. It was infested with roaches. I was always bombing the place and made sure to keep it extra clean. Overall, I was grateful that we had a roof over our heads. I made our house a happy little home. I remember praying daily for God to send his angels to protect us from all the hurt, harm, and danger. I also prayed daily that He would make a way for us to move to a better neighborhood one day. I would hear gunshots often, and a young man was killed right outside of our apartment building. I stayed in the house, and I did not keep much company. I soon became aware that someone was secretly harassing me. When I would arrive home, I would find that someone had urinated right in front of my door. At first, I thought it was an accident, but it kept happening. I became frightened, and I began to earnestly pray that God would watch over us before this person actually would try to harm us.

A couple weeks later, I learned that a program was having a lottery drawing, and they would be putting working families in decent affordable housing. I picked up several applications and filled out at least three. I also passed them out to other single mothers, hoping that all of us could live in a more decent environment. I new the waiting list was very long, and I heard that some people had to wait up to ten years to move. I remember taking my applications to the mailbox. Before I dropped it in, I asked God to allow one of His angels to carry my application to the top of the waiting list so we could move from our environment.

A few months later, the people whom I gave applications to informed me that they had been placed on the waiting list. I began to grow sad because I had not heard anything. I at least wanted to be on the waiting list with everyone else. I remember a little voice encouraged my spirit and told me not to worry because God saw that I tried to help others, and because I gave others applications unselfishly when I did not have to, He would not forget about me.

A couple weeks later, I lay asleep and dreamt I went out to the mailbox and received a letter stating that I was moving. I saw myself dancing, laughing, and shouting, "I am moving out the projects!"

I awoke and wondered if it was true. I told my girlfriend the dream, and she laughed. Approximately one week later, I was collecting my mail and found a letter in my mailbox. I was happy and expected them to inform me that I was placed on the waiting list. When I opened the letter, it was a congratulation letter, informing me that I had been chosen as one of the families to receive affordable decent housing.

My heart was overjoyed and sure enough, I was shouting, dancing, and screaming that I was moving out the projects! This was a real blessing. I knew that God really heard my prayer that day I asked Him to send His angel to put my application at the top of the list, and that is just what He did. I remember I promised God that if He would make a way for me to move, I would go back to school and peruse my education. God kept His promise to me, and I was going to definitely keep my promise to him. What would I go to school for? I knew in my heart that I always wanted to be a doctor. At the time, I did not have enough confidence to convince myself that I could become a doctor. I decided to become a Pharmacist. I applied to college and was on my way towards success.

One night I prayed and I asked God if becoming a pharmacist was what he desired for me, and if not, to tell me what He wanted me to be. A few nights later, I lay asleep, and I saw myself dressed in a white jacket with a stethoscope around my neck. My hair was cut in a pretty style, and I had some diamond studs on. Most of all, I gleamed with radiance, and I was smiling from ear to ear. When I awoke the next morning, I had made up in my mind; I would become a Christian physician.

Therefore, I began one of the most difficult challenges I ever faced. I had not been to school since high school and that was over eight years. Studying the sciences was very hard. I would stay up all night and still mess up on my exams. I would cry after each exam, because it seemed like the material I reviewed for the exam was not actually on the exam. Shortly after I started attending college, I met a young woman who was a student at Morehouse School of Medicine. She was working towards her Ph.D. in the biomedical sciences. Her name is Terry Moore. She took the responsibility of becoming my mentor and agreed to allow me to research the disease, chlamydia, under the supervision of her head mentor. I was a freshman in college and had not even finished my first biology class, and here I was doing extensive research.

I remember crying my first day at Morehouse. I felt stupid. Everyone kept using big words, and I was intimidated. Terry taught me from the basics. She would sit me down and drill the sciences in my head. I would get frustrated with her, and I know her patience was running thin with me. She was like a big sister to me and really made an impact in my life. Day after day, I would go to Morehouse and learn science. They had me washing cells, dissecting lymph nodes from mice, counting cells, writing scientific papers, and developing poster boards to take on trips. The program was known as RISE. Boy did I rise. I began to understand what people were talking about when we would go to conference meetings. I began to get better grades in my science classes, and because of the complicated scientific abstracts I learned to develop, I was making A's in my English classes. I began to feel like a scientist. I began to feel intelligent.

I thank God for the experience at Morehouse School of Medicine, and I know that I would not have been able to pass my science classes if I had not been excepted into the RISE program. Wonderful things can be brought forth from our dreams. Because of a dream, I gained enough courage to take on the challenge of learning new things. I would have never had this wonderful opportunity to fill my mind with the wonderful mysteries of science if I had not followed the vision of myself in my dream. I would not have had the courage at least to try to be what I always desired if I had not dreamed.

I believe when we follow and pursue our dreams, our lives change for the better. Dreams of healing, success, warnings, revelation, and prosperity are all dreams that have meaning. Silly dreams are even satisfying too. We all need to dream. If God revealed things to the heroes of the bible, are we not the as they were? Children of God? God will speak to us in the form of dreams and visions, and it is up to us to have enough faith to receive the things that He reveals to us. God will never forsake us or lead us to do ungodly things. If you dream you killed someone, for crying out loud, do not make that dream a reality. That is not a vision from God. That is of the devil! However, begin to fulfill the good dreams. If you dream you are singing, work up some confidence and some courage to go sign up for a talent show. You never know who may be there watching and waiting to discover you. If you dream that you're in the Bahamas relaxing and drinking fruity drinks, go ahead and take a vacation. If you dream of an old friend, call that person just to say hello and let them know your thinking of them. Make your dreams come true.

God will speak things that bring peace to your soul. God will show you visions to warn you of harm and danger. God will send angels to you to speak answers to the things we pray about. God will speak healing to your soul while you lay sleep. You may go to bed asking God for direction and wake up the next morning with an answer. If He revealed things to people in the bible, He will reveal things to you too! He is the same yesterday, today, and forever more. It is however our responsibility to believe in the God we serve, ourselves, and our dreams enough to actually get up and make them manifest into reality.

When we dream, life becomes exciting. When we dream our spiritual walk becomes an adventure. When we begin to manifest our dreams, our circumstances begin to change. I have learned to believe in my dreams. When we have dreams that consistently heal us, change the way we live, and lead us into a courageous, adventurous, faith filled life, we are then walking in the purpose that God created us to walk. Some say it's foolish to chase fantasies, but it is through fantasies, visions, and dreams that we are able to talk on the phone, drive automobiles, live in mansions, ride roller coasters at amusement parks, eat ice cream, and do all of the other wonders that have been birthed onto this planet by the dreams and visions that God has revealed to others. What dreams has God revealed to you? Have you ignored them? Have you made an effort to manifest your dreams? If you have not, I encourage you to begin to follow your dreams.

Speak these words to affirm your God given dreams:

Today, I will now begin to make my dreams become reality. Today, I will learn to believe in the things that I dream. As I lie down to sleep, I will hear from God the things He would say to me. I will believe in the things that He reveals to me. I am now a receptive and willing vessel for God my creator to communicate with me. In Jesus' name, it is done.

31. Affirmation Affirming Spiritual Balance

Let me be weighed in an even balance, that God may know mine integrity (Job 31:6).

One day after I had almost driven my self nuts trying to figure out what was the truth about life and what was not the truth about life, I realized that it was time for me to come to some sort of conclusion for myself. I could no longer believe what others told me, but I had to begin to examine every situation life was presenting me and learn the truth from it. When we fail to try to understand our own truth about life, we then open the door for an imbalanced spirit, confusion, and a lifetime of uncertainty.

Everyone experiences life differently, and I knew that I could never discover my truth about life based on someone else's opinion. I think the biggest truth that I needed to discover was my beliefs about God. I believed that for most of my life, I was misinformed about God. I could not understand why my cousin, at the age of thirteen, became pregnant by a minister at our church, who was twice her age. I could not understand why my aunt, who was so holy, forced me tell a lie on an innocent young man. She forced me to lie and say he sexually molested me. I kept on telling her this young man never touched me, but she told me if I did not say he violated me she was going to hurt me. I was only about nine at the time, and her brothers and her son had already sexually abused me. So, I knew when someone violated me or not. But, I feared her. Her beatings were brutal. All I could think about was being beat all over with a high heel shoe, an extension cord, or having my jaw pulled out of its socket. Therefore, I said what she forced me to say. How could a woman of God force a young child to tell such a lie?

The young man lived down the street and our families socialized frequently. He and I liked each other, but it was innocent. He never once laid a hand on me. He never once insinuated any sexual act with me. We never even talked about it. We played as two children should play. My aunt ruined everything. The young man went under investigation for nothing. I knew for years that he was deeply hurt. I was also hurt. I saw him one day shortly after all the drama. He looked at me almost in tears and said, "Melissa, you know I never did anything to you."

I looked at him sadly, held my head down, and did not say a word because I was so afraid if I said anything, my aunt would hurt me. For years, I always knew the truth. I could no longer play with them, and every time his brothers and sisters would see me, they would taunt me and call me a liar. This deeply scarred me, and I always hoped to see him as an adult so that I could ask his forgiveness. Did all people who serve God force children to tell lies on other people? Did all ministers who serve God impregnate young girls and leave them to raise children alone? As a child, I made up in my mind; I would one day discover the truth. Growing up in the church, I had been told about all the things I was going to the flames of hell for and all the things that would get me through the gates of heaven. I was told that God was someone who punished people when they do bad things.

I remember one evening my father brought us to a prayer meeting at his church. I remember walking through the doors and this woman came up to me and asked me to sit down. When I sat down, she asked me with the kindest voice, "Do you want to go to hell for coming into the house of the Lord with those pants on?"

I said calmly with an embarrassing look on my face, "No."

She then politely asked me not to come to church with pants on ever again. I never understood why God would send me to hell for wearing a pair of pants to church, but I knew better than to question her.

This woman became very fond of me. She took me shopping and bought me skirts and dresses to wear to church. She began to spend a lot of time with me, and I grew to respect and love her dearly. This church was also against going to the movies. The pastor would tell the parents that our minds would be poisoned with the filth of the world. My dad would not take us to the movies nor would he let us go with friends. I was also told that only women who have the spirit of Jezebel enjoy wearing makeup.

As you can see, they told me many things. I always longed for the truth. Would God really send me to hell if I decided to go to the movies? Was I wicked like Jezebel If I decided to wear makeup? I knew this was a bunch of crap. When the time came for me to awaken to the truth about God and the things He liked and disliked, the only conclusion I made was that God is a God who loves me so much and requires me to do the same. He is a God who takes pleasure in obedience. The most beautiful thing I discovered about God was that He judged men according to the contents of their hearts. I discovered what this actually meant. It actually meant that I must have a good heart, because if my heart was good than I would do good things. I also learned that God loved those who did good for others and themselves.

How did I find out about God? I remember thinking if I were to become friends with God, I must know what He likes and what He dislikes. I began to study the bible, and I discovered so many things about God. My studies became so deep that I discovered that God really loved sweet aromas. I wanted to please God so much that I began to buy sweet smelling incense and pure frankincense and myrrh. I would pray and ask God to please enjoy the sweet smell I was burning just for Him. I also found that He was a God of emotion. He gets sad, He gets angry, and He can be happy just as we can. I know all this sounds extreme, but my ultimate goal was to touch the soft spot in God's heart so that He would know that I really loved Him and because of my love for Him, I hoped that He would always remember me and watch over me. I felt good because I was beginning to become acquainted with the one who created me. I felt as though

I could tell him anything. I could tell him the good things and the bad things because He knew everything anyway.

All the misconceptions I had been told began to fade away because I was building a relationship with God, and He was beginning to fill me with knowledge, wisdom, and truth. I now understand that because I had been misinformed about God, for years I was spiritually imbalanced. Because I chose to try to establish a bond and friendship with Him, He, little by little and step by step, began to even me.

If you have been taught misconceptions about God, do not feel bad. Do not blame anyone. Most people only repeat what they have been taught. It is kind of like a cycle. Somebody told your momma's momma, so your mother told you, and you probably will tell your children only the things that you were taught. I will not write and tell you what you should believe about God because that would take away from your personal experience with him. It is crucial that each of us become intimate with God. If we do not, we will never know the truth about who He really is for ourselves.

An important type of imbalance is spiritual imbalance in the Christian churches. This is a very sensitive topic to discuss, because I know some will be offended. However, I have been free from people-bondage for quite some time, and if I step on a few toes, oh well. The truth sets us free. The name of this book is *Healing Affirmations for the Wounded Soul*, and in order for healing to take place, our souls must be set free by the truth. I have discovered so many Christians are spiritually imbalanced because they lack the truth about God. They have attended church all their lives only to discover they have not changed one bit. These spiritually imbalanced souls have not brought forth one branch of good fruit. Why? The answer is that these individuals never took the time to get to know God on an intimate level. They never made an effort to examine their hearts and minds, probably because they have been too busy examining everyone else's hearts and minds. These people I call spiritually imbalanced souls.

Spiritually imbalanced souls spend a whole lot of time in the house of God finding out everyone's business and spreading it around by pretending to ask prayer for them. Spiritually imbalanced souls spend all their time in church trying to be seen and recognized for their busy-ness to win the approval of others when on the inside they are spiritually nuts. You may see these people every time the doors of the house of God open. I do not care how much a person loves God; it is unhealthy to be involved in so many activities at church that you deprive yourself of rest and a social life.

God had enough sense to get rest, and so did Jesus. Jesus often escaped to a place of quietness so that He could rest properly. Spiritually imbalanced souls end up burned out and feel depleted. When this happens, they begin to blame others for their burn out. Spiritually imbalanced souls judge other people, they pass unfair judgments on everyone who tries to do good, they gossip, they despise their leader, they are jealous when others get blessed, and they smile in your face knowing that they secretly hate you on the inside.

It is no mystery why they are imbalanced. They are imbalanced because they are doing everything but getting closer to God. I am fully aware the church is indeed a spiritual hospital. However, I also understand that hospitals are designed to help sick people get well so they can go back home. The church is a spiritual hospital designed to help sick souls become well so they can go home to be with Jesus one day. There is spiritual imbalance when people are getting worse in the house of God instead of getting better.

When a person is sick enough to the point where he or she has to be hospitalized, the doctors and other team members give the sick person medicine, and usually the person gets better with time. This is how it is suppose to be in our churches. People may come in with negative attitudes, but within a short time, they should begin to change. In other words, their spirits should be getting well. The atmosphere of the church should contribute to their spiritual healing. People may come into the church with habits that are not pleasing to God, however within time, their behaviors should be shaping into behavior that is pleasing to the Lord.

Why are so many ministries being destroyed? Why are people spreading AIDS to one another in the house of God? Why are once highly esteemed leaders falling and turning away from God? Everyone blames their behaviors on Satan. I believe Satan can only present us with ideas. It is up to us to be balanced enough in our spirits to refuse to act on any and every idea he presents. Spiritual balance must be found in every church and in every human being. How do you balance your spirit?

It is all up to us to discover what lies deep with in our hearts. What is in the heart of man will eventually show throughout his daily activities. Spiritual balance falls into place when we allow the fruits of the spirit to come forth. When we daily bring forth the fruits of the spirit, we begin to even out. When we practice love in all situations, love begins to fill our spirits and we actually do not have enough room in our hearts for hatred. We must also learn to make time to do things that we have to do, like to do, and need to do.

Another important thing to know is that nothing or no one can ever separate you from God's love. You are always connected to God because you breathe. Every time you inhale and exhale, you are in God's presence. God lives inside of you and will never stop loving you no matter what. So many religions teach that God will love you if you do this, but if you do that, you can have no part of God. Always remember as long as you are breathing you are a part of God. When you die God will be there. God is everywhere all the time. If you do not seek God for yourself, you will have no other choice but to be spiritually nuts. You will never be sure of your relationship with God or yourself. You will never fully understand just how much God really loves you.

Have you ever known someone who you saw regularly in church and then they'd disappear for a while before returning? To us this is known as backsliding or turning your back on God. I like to call it spiritual imbalance. Somehow, this individual cannot grasp the concept that even if he did or did not walk with God, God would always love him. This individual person believes that when he makes a mistake and commits a fault, he is no longer worthy to be in God's presence. He feels he should not come to church anymore because he simply cannot live a perfect life that he believes he has to live for God. This is why so many people stay away from the church. I know this because I was one of these people. I quit going to church because I made mistakes. I thought I could not have a relationship with God because I was sexually active without being married. It was indeed wrong, however, I should have had enough sense to know that if I kept going to church and asking God for help, he would soon deliver me somehow. I did not know that if I kept on seeking God, He would eventually awaken the seed of love inside of me so that I would one day understand the true purpose in love making. Every wrong thing I did kept me from having a personal experience with God (at least this is what I thought).

One day, I decided to dedicate my life to God. I was left to raise two beautiful children all alone, and I knew that if no one else would help me, God would. I remember praying and telling God these words, *"Lord, I have always loved you, and I have always desired to have a relationship with you. However, I cannot serve you if I always feel you are going to punish me when I mess up. Can't you just love me the way I am? Can't we be friends even though I make mistakes? Can't we have a relationship even though my life is a mess? Lord, as of today, I am going to stay with you. If I sin, I will ask for your forgiveness and try to do better. However, I have to know that you love me no matter what I do, because if I do not feel that you love me, then I will never be able to walk consistently in your presence. So I will live for you based on one condition, that you promise to never stop loving me."*

Ever since that day, I have steadfastly remained friends with God. I decided, through the good and the bad, through thick and sin, I would work my salvation out with God. To be honest, I have made a mistake every day since I said that prayer. A day has not gone by that I have not messed up. But guess what? My life has still changed, my heart has still changed, and I have learned to pull even closer to God through all my mess ups. This was my first and most important step to balancing my spirit, understanding that God would always love me, and if I would just stick with him, He would change me. I look back now at situations that I used to cry over and now I laugh, smile, and thank God for loving me through it all.

My grandfather did not believe that he needed to take any medications. The doctors informed him that he had several severe medical conditions that would eventually cost him his life. He did not care what they told him, he simply refused to take his medications. He believed that God would heal him supernaturally. Years down the line, he became severely ill and died. I understood that it must have been his time to go, however, I could not see why he would not take his medication. As a mature adult, I now understand that my grandfather was spiritually imbalanced. He did love God and was a pretty righteous guy, however he failed to understand that the many different medicines that science has developed were actually put inside different plants by God to help sick people get well and live longer.

God knew when He created us that down the road there would be many different diseases and sicknesses that would cut short the lives of many. God knew that our brains were brilliant enough to one day discover the secrets to healing through medicine in the leaves of plants and trees. I also understand that God has the healing power within His hands and all He has to do is command healing to a sickness and that sickness would be destroyed; yet this does not happen to everyone and is not meant to happen to everyone.

Some have been healed supernaturally by God's power, and some have been healed through the practice of medicine. Regardless of how an individual recovers from sickness, the important thing is that they are no longer ill. When a person is diagnosed with cancer, he has a choice. He can get medical treatment or he can refuse medical treatment. The choice is his to make. A person who refuses medical treatment and decides to believe in God for healing has every right to do so after all it is his right to choose. I believe it is always wise to get medical treatment and begin to pray that God will send his healing power through the means of the treatment or supernaturally. Prayer and medical treatment are an excellent source of healing. After all, everything belongs to God, and if He did not want us to take medicine than He would not have created plants that contain healing for so many diseases nor would he have put it in our minds to seek healing through plants and leaves.

You are spiritually imbalanced if you do not go for regular medical checkups. You are spiritually imbalanced if you do not except medical treatment based on religious beliefs. I know this is tough, but someone has to tell the truth. The truth is God has anointed certain people to specialize in healthcare. He has ordained doctors, surgeons, dentists, and other specialist to ensure that you stay healthy so that you may enjoy your days here on earth. I have always believed that a doctor, whether he believes in God or not, is always surrounded by angels of healing and wisdom. Doctors need extra knowledge and wisdom to make important decisions about medical treatments and important decisions about your health.

Ben Carson is a world-renowned surgeon who I adore. He has saved the lives of many children, and he has never been so proud to say that he has only done so with the help of God. I enjoyed reading all of his books, in which he continuously admits that there has been times in the operating room when patients actually have flat-lined. He then called on Jesus for wisdom and instruction on what to do and because he asked God for direction, their lives were saved. It can only be a special blessing from God to be able to hold a steady hand to go into the brain and save someone's life. It takes an anointed hand to actually open the human heart and perform different procedures that will help it beat properly. It is a gift from God to have doctors that specialize in treating human disease.

Many lives are saved every day due to medicine. Of course, we all know that God has the final say so in whether people live or die. Often, some people can receive the best medical treatment there is and yet die. When this happens, we all know that it is the person's appointed time to leave this world. I only wish people would not be so imbalanced that they will not at least try to seek medical treatment for their conditions. God holds the power to perform miracles and He will do so if He chooses to, but wisdom encourages us to visit the doctor on a regular basis to ensure that we stay healthy.

When you are spiritually balanced, you know within your heart who God is and no one will ever be able to make you think anything that exalts itself against God. When you are spiritually balanced, you make time each day to do a little bit of everything. When you are spiritually balanced, you understand that you must tell others no sometimes. When you are spiritually balanced, you understand that you cannot be involved in every single ministry offered at church. When you are spiritually balanced, you understand that not every thing is of the devil. When you are spiritually balanced, you do not go around trying to please everyone. When you are spiritually balanced, you see people as God sees people, as special creations learning through the mistakes they make to become more like their father in heaven. When you are spiritually balanced, you no longer care what other people say about you behind your back. When you are spiritually balanced, you make time for yourself. When you are spiritually balanced, you make time for those who are important to you. When you are spiritually balanced, you understand that everything happens for a reason, in its own timing, and all for God's glory.

Are you spiritually imbalanced? It is okay if you do not want to tell me. Please tell God and tell yourself the truth. It can be very difficult to accept that you may be spiritually imbalanced, but look at it this way. If you never become aware of the imbalance in your life, then how will you work to improve it? Go ahead; confess this affirmative prayer with me so that you may be healed of spiritual imbalance:

Speak these words of balance into your life today!

I am now bringing my mind and my spirit into balance. I am even in all areas of my life. My mind and my spirit are in harmony. I will love, for this is balance. I will learn, for this is balance. I will rest, for this is balance. I will say no when necessary, for this is balance. I will see others as God sees them, for this is balance. I will make time for my loved ones, for this is balance. I will make time for me. Nothing can ever separate me from the love of God, for knowing this is balance. I will take care of me, for this is true balance. I will see a doctor for regular check ups, for this is balance. I will make time for prayer and meditation, for this is balance. I will enjoy my days under the sun, for this is balance. Thank you God for balance in my life. In Jesus' name, it is done.

32. Affirmation of Healing

In the mist of the street of it, and of either side of the river, was there a tree of life, which bare twelve manner of fruits, and yielded her fruit every month: and the leaves of the tree were for the healing of the nations (Revelation 22:2).

There is healing for your soul loved one. All the hurt and pain you have experienced in your life was brought about to bring you closer to me. I have loved you with an everlasting love and with everlasting mercy. Allow the healing balm of my leaves to soothe your soul. Let my words of healing flow throughout your spirit man. Pain, sickness, sorrow, and tears shall be no more. I have come that you may have life and have it more abundantly, that in me you may be made whole and live. Be thou well my child. Be thou at peace, and most of all be free. For I am that tree that stands in the mist of the street. For it is I who bears the fruits of healing. Eat there of my fruit and you shall be full, says the Lord your God.

Jesus, the River of Life

There was a time in my life that I was down and out. I had so many troubles, I felt trapped with no way out. All of my problems, I tried to solve them, all of my fears, I looked for others to calm them, but when I met Jesus, I met the river of life.

The river of life flows so freely, Jesus came that I may have life and have it abundantly. The river of life flows so freely, flowing from the throne of God with Jesus, coursing down the main stream.

There was a time I was blind and could not see. A time when addiction, affliction, and all my sins, hindered me. Then one day I saw the beautiful light shining and it was so brilliantly bright that it opened my eyes. For this was the day that I met Jesus, the river of life. Thank you heavenly father for setting my soul free. (Melissa Jones)

When our past wounds us, we must look to God for healing. So many of us look to others to make us feel like were healed and whole, but it is only in God's love that we can find healing. No man or woman can ever make you feel as God can make you feel. People can only offer each other temporary comforts, but God offers a comfort that will last throughout eternal life. God will complete you, fill you, and make you whole. I encourage you loved one to begin to confront the hurts of your past and accept them as part of you. Grieve for a while. Extract the truths you have learned. Cry if you must. Allow God to heal your wounds of the past so you can glide into your future with success. Do not be afraid or ashamed of your past, but use your past as a testimony to help another broken soul heal from his or her wounded past.

Speak these words of healing into your life today:

For today, I am healed. For today, I am whole. For today, I am free. I am healed; in Jesus' name, it is done!

33. The Meaning of Life

In ending this book, I wrote from my spirit God's perspective of life. Sometime ago, I recorded these words in my journal, and I hope they will be a blessing to your spirit as they were to mine. I pray that you have been richly blessed by reading this book, and I pray that God's blessing of transformation and change be upon every soul that comes in contact and repeats the anointed affirmations written in this book.

Spirit Speaks:

Seasons come and go. Life is full of its ups and its downs. The weather may change but I the Lord God never change. You must live and you must learn. As you live and learn, you grow, as do the flowers. I designed the human mind for this purpose. Some choose to ignore their season for growth and change, yet some embrace this season. Whatever you decide to do my dear child, my presence will forever be with thee. You will never be able to fully understand the creation of mankind, but the spirit himself knows and does. I have given man freewill. I will that every man lives a meaningful and purpose filled life. It is however man's choice how and what he chooses to do while here on earth.

My love never fails regardless of what you decide. This is where I am ever merciful towards man. It saddens me to see a life wasted, a life lived without purpose. But free will must always abide as long as man exists and will never be taken away from him. If I interfered with the choices that you make that would prove me a liar, which I can never be. I do however present you with a choice to choose, that which is good or to choose that which is evil. So understand this my child, there is no such thing as failure because you are destined by the choices that you make. Life is but a special moment for man. Life is a preparation of lessons for the journey into eternal bliss that each soul I created must take at his appointed time. Embrace life and be ye not discouraged. Do not be dismayed at the things you have done in the past but begin this day to choose that which is wise. Begin to love at all times. Make each day a beautiful and meaningful day. I have given thee the power to do so.

Printed in the United States
26207LVS00001B/361